the handbook of
Smoothies
and Juicing

the handbook of
Smoothies
and Juicing

Judith Millidge

BARNES
& NOBLE
BOOKS
NEW YORK

This edition published by Barnes & Noble, Inc.,
By arrangement with D&S Books Ltd

2004 Barnes & Noble Books

M 10 9 8 7 6 5 4 3 2

ISBN 0-7607-5662-7

Creative Director: Sarah King
Editor: Sarah Harris
Project Editor: Yvonne Worth
Photographer: Colin Bowling
Designer: Axis Design

© 2003 D&S Books Ltd

Printed in China

Contents

The Joy of Juicing

For decades, health professionals have been telling us to consume more fresh fruit and vegetables, that we are clogging our arteries with unhealthy fats and too much protein. This sensible advice is matched by that found in the plethora of books, magazines, and websites ranging from the straightforward to the frankly outlandish – that the secret of immortality can be found in becoming a lettuce-munching born-again juice fanatic. There must be happy medium and this book is it.

Freshly juiced oranges provide a thick and surprisingly creamy juice.

While it explains the nutritional value of fruit and vegetables, it promotes the belief that juice and smoothie recipes are here to be enjoyed – if your personal tastes do not extend to spinach juice, don't drink it (although it's nicer than you might think). Similarly, the detox recipes and those intended to enhance the health of certain parts of the body are also there to be enjoyed for themselves – the fact that they might do you good is an extra benefit.

It is said that no-one dies wishing they had spent longer at the office and although it seems unlikely that anyone has ever expired wishing they had eaten more green vegetables, it would be a shame to die tragically young of a heart attack, with your last thought dwelling on the question of whether it could have been avoided by downing just one fresh smoothie instead of a beer and pretzels.

A state-of-the-art centrifugal juicer.

What's in a name?

Smoothies and juices are very similar, not to say indistinguishable – it's all a question of terminology. Juicing is a great way to incorporate fresh produce into your diet, but there is something slightly more hedonistic about smoothies. Smoothies often include milk, cream, ice cream or yogurt – scrumptious, sweet additions which perfectly complement and enhance the tang of fresh juice. They can also incorporate herbs and spices, such as ginger, cinnamon, parsley or rosemary, or honey for added sweetness. Children, in particular, enjoy the addition of cocoa or grated chocolate to make elaborate smoothie shakes. By adding crushed ice or even fizzy drinks, you can

expand your repertoire even further – even branch out into the realm of cocktails: some, like the classic pina colada, taste great with a shot of rum or vodka.

Smoothies can be made in a blender, simply by chopping the fruit, removing skin and pits and blending it all to a pulp. Additional ingredients can be added to the blender and – presto ! – your drink is ready. In this way, the whole fruit can be consumed, fiber, juice ,and all. In addition to the health-giving vitamins and enzymes, you will consume the fruit's fiber, which is excellent for the health of the colon and bowel.

Juicing, however, is the extraction of the juice from a fruit or vegetable, leaving behind the fruit's fiber and pulp in the juicer. In this way, the raw nutrients of the fruit or vegetable, the vitamins, minerals, sugars, starches, and enzymes, form a concentrate of almost all the plant's nutrients, without the fibrous plant cell walls. This juice can be absorbed quickly and easily by the body, without the bother of digesting pulp. Almost all fruit and vegetables are suitable for juicing, although some vegetables such as broccoli or cauliflower, are rather bitter and are more palatable once mixed with a sweeter ingredient, such a carrot or apple juice.

A glass of colorful, fresh, tangy fruit juice is hard to resist and strangely, freshly juiced fruit is quite unlike the juice that emerges from chilled cartons. Natural juices appear quite creamy: freshly-juiced orange, for example, is almost an apricot color, because the pith is juiced along with the pulp.

While juicing is a valuable part of a balanced diet, it is not the answer to all our dietary ills, but it can make a significant difference to health, vitality and looks. Remember that juice lacks fiber, fat, and protein which are also vital to maintain energy and preserve optimum health. Smoothies, on the other hand, can provide a bulkier drink and, with the addition of milk-based ingredients, often incorporate the nutrients missing from a simple juice. Smoothies, in particular, are often a vital and enjoyable part of an invalid diet for those too ill to cope with solid food.

Both smoothies and juices enable you to consume fresh produce in its raw state, with the nutrients intact. Cooking is thought to destroy many essential amino acids, vitamins, and minerals which are so vital to a well-balanced diet and which protect the body against illness. Furthermore, it is easier for the body to assimilate nutritious liquid than solid matter, so the goodness inherent in fruit and vegetables is processed more quickly by the digestive system. Fresh juices and smoothies will certainly boost your overall health, provide better resistance to disease and possibly clear up minor complaints. Best of all they taste great and are easy to prepare!

Juicing pioneers

The ancient Greeks realized that, to an extent, you are what you eat: "Each one of the substances of a man's diet acts upon his body and changes it in some way, and upon these changes his whole life depends, whether he be in health, sickness or convalescent." Hippocrates' words have never found a more receptive audience than today, when many people believe that the essential nutrients in much of our food have been depleted by modern farming techniques

The White Stuff

Cows' milk is a first class protein, an excellent source of calcium, and contains B vitamins and traces of iron and zinc. Even in its full-cream form, the fat content is a mere 4%; a 250mg glass contains less than 5g of fat. This is not a problem for children, who should not be given low fat milk (it lacks the vitamins A, D, and E which are present in whole milk), but some adults may prefer to use skimmed or low-fat milk in their smoothies.

and modern food production and distribution. Blending and juicing fresh fruit and vegetables, preferably using organic produce, is one way to regain the natural goodness lost to the gods of profit, preservation, and expediency.

The idea of feeding raw produce to patients in order to improve their overall health emerged at the end of the 19th century, interestingly at a time when the very earliest convenience foods were beginning to permeate the market. The introduction of canning in the middle of the 19th century made a huge difference to the diet of travellers, explorers, and especially, soldiers, who for the first time could rely on reasonably tasty, well-preserved food, rather than depending on what they could scavenge on their travels. This was the beginning of the slippery slope whereby freshness was sacrificed to convenience. Canned foods undoubtedly filled a need, but 150 years later, it is arguable that we have come to rely too much on food that has had the natural goodness processed out of it.

Smoothies made with dairy products have two advantages: they add valuable calcium to the diet, and retain the fiber inherent in the vegetables and fruit. Women especially need to maintain a steady intake of calcium, as hormonal changes deplete calcium reserves over time, leading to a reduction in bone mass, brittle bones and an increased risk of osteoporosis. With the right ingredients, a smoothie can be a meal in itself,

perfect for an invalid, or a variety of diets – get the mix right and you can use smoothies for weight gain or weight loss!

Smoothies, or juices made in a blender, retain the fibrous parts of the fruit and vegetables and this fiber is an essential part of everyone's diet, as it helps maintain the health of the lower bowel.

Some fruits, notably bananas and small berries, are more suited to blenders than juicers, but if you prefer to juice your fruit rather than blend it, you can still make use of the fruit pulp. You must use it immediately, or freeze it, as left in a fridge it oxidizes and deteriorates very quickly. Fruit pulp can be used in baking, ice-cream-making, soup recipes or as part of a salad. You can even use it to make face masks and beauty treatments. Fruits which contain proteolytic enzymes are excellent skin cleansers, so if you find yourself with leftover kiwi, pineapple, mango or papaya pulp, smear it over you face, lie down for ten minutes, then wash it off.

Juicing combinations

Although smoothies and juices usually taste far better when made with fresh fruit, the use of commercial juice is sometimes unavoidable, and, particularly if you are catering for several people, it can be far more convenient. There is no harm or shame in mixing up a smoothie or juice using a combination of fresh produce and juice from a carton – it often makes the whole process easier.

Nature vs Nurture in your diet

It is widely acknowledged that many of us in Western societies do not eat enough fresh produce. Nutritionists recommend the consumption of five portions of fruit and vegetables a day in order to provide a balanced intake of vitamins and minerals as part of a healthy diet. Many people fall a long way short of these minimum recommendations: in the U.S.A., for example, the average person manages one and a half portions, and in Britain, 65 percent of the population eat only one item. Scientific studies have proved that eating more fresh produce significantly reduces the risk of early death from heart disease or cancer.

There are few of us who do not eat at least some processed and refined food, and the great majority of people probably do not eat what nutritionists regard as enough fruit and vegetables. It is an omission that is all too easy to ignore, as we whiz from one appointment to another, with barely time to grab a snack, never mind a well-balanced meal. The health of many people is undermined by their frenetic lifestyle and the stress of trying to keep too many balls in the air, balancing the demands of work and family. It is not surprising that many of us fall prey to a recurring range of minor ailments, some of which can build up and lead to more serious illnesses.

Fresh fruit and vegetables are vital ingredients in every diet. They provide vitamins and minerals that help protect the body against a range of disorders and diseases, from the common cold to cancer. They are cheap, easily available, portable (in the case of most types of fruit), delicious, and ideal snack food, so why don't we eat enough? Why do we fill ourselves up with sugary cakes and greasy fries instead? The answer, of course, is that they provide a quick fix, satisfying the appetite while doing almost nothing valuable in a nutritional way.

Incorporating fresh juice into your diet will not only make you more healthy, but the very process of taking time to prepare juice will allow you time to slow down, relax, and reflect upon your life. You could augment your health with any number of vitamin supplements, but juicing the right ingredients can prove to be more effective. Juicing enables you to absorb more of the goodness of fresh produce than if you ate the whole fruit or vegetable. It is a rare person who would consider eating a whole pineapple at one sitting, but a 8 fl oz (225 ml) glass of juice, made from one pineapple, is a far more palatable prospect. Juicing fresh vegetables is especially effective, as cooking destroys many of the proteins and nutrients, whereas juicing preserves them intact. Fresh juices are easy to digest, although, because they lack fiber, they should not entirely replace your intake of fruit and vegetables. (Fiber is essential for lower bowel health.) The enzymes present in fresh produce work with the body's enzymes to break down the juice and absorb its goodness into the bloodstream within minutes of being consumed.

Another common shortcoming in many Western diets is the comparative drought that exists in our fluid intake. The human body is a fluid construction: 70 percent of our frames consist of water, and it must be replenished or we will suffer from dehydration. We lose 2.5 pints (1.5 liters) a day through sweating and waste excretion. In order to keep ourselves functioning at the optimum level of fitness, adults should drink at least 4 pints (1 liter) of water a day, but this should be in addition to caffeinated drinks such as tea, coffee, or cola. In processing many of the ingredients in carbonated drinks, tea or coffee, the body actually uses water; furthermore, these drinks have a diuretic effect and do not replenish the body's fluid supplies. Fresh fruit and vegetables are packed with water and their juice is not only tastier than plain water, but it is loaded with vital ingredients for health. Scientists have found that brain efficiency is improved in people who consume more water and fresh juice, so if you find yourself slumping at your desk in the early afternoon, treat yourself to some fresh juice instead of a soda, and watch your efficiency levels rise!

Greens are good for you!

Fruit and vegetables contain an extremely wide range of vitamins and minerals, but are especially rich in betacarotene (which the body converts to vitamin A), vitamin C, potassium and phosphorus. Vitamins make the enzymes within the body work, firing up the processes that convert food into energy. They help maintain the body's hormonal balance, boost the immune system, and are vital for the working of the brain and the nervous system. Minerals are also vital to the smooth functioning of the human body. The body can not produce minerals and so they must be absorbed from food. Calcium and magnesium are found in vegetables such as kale, cabbage, and root vegetables, and the chlorophyll in green vegetables helps protect the nervous system and build muscles. Brightly colored fruit and vegetables, such as beetroot, tomatoes, and berries derive their color from flavonoids, powerful antioxidants, which combat aging and many degenerative diseases such as cancer.

Equipment: juicers, blenders and other gadgets

One reason for the increasing popularity of juicing in recent years is the introduction of efficient, affordable electric juicers. The prospect of mashing fruit and laboriously pushing it through a sieve is enough to put off even the most ardent convert, but, fortunately, there are many different juicers on the market that do the job extremely quickly and will suit a range of budgets. It is important to remember that a juicer works very differently from a blender, which simply purees the fruit and fiber together. A juicer separates the fiber from the juice, to give a smooth, easily digestible liquid.

Juicing does not need to become an expensive fad. All you really need to produce fresh citrus juice are simple lemon squeezers like these.

The most basic juicer is probably already in your kitchen – the humble lemon squeezer. All citrus fruits can be squeezed efficiently, quickly and extremely cheaply using one of these. They are available in a number of forms, from the most basic plastic version, through more sophisticated two-handed items that increase the pressure on the fruit, up to the beautiful creation designed by Philippe Starcke.

Many food processors include a juicing attachment, which makes the job of squeezing lots of oranges for a morning juice much easier. Some processors also have a blade for juice extraction, which works in the same way as a centrifugal juicer. Most incorporate a blender as well, although of course, stand-alone blenders are easily available. So, if you are unsure about whether to dip your toes into the colorful waters of juicing, try mixing up a few citrus cocktails for a few days and whisking them with some mashed banana for a quick taste of the sun.

Hand-held blenders have the virtue of being small and easy to store, and the

Electric juicers, such as these centrifugal machines, are now available in a range of sizes and colors to match your budget, lifestyle ,and kitchen decor.

more expensive incorporate ice crushers. They are often dishwasher-proof, too! More robust blenders have a capacity of about 3 pints (1.5 liters). The higher the wattage, the faster and more powerful the machine, so look for one with about 400 watts of power that advertizes its ice-crushing ability. There are also hybrid blenders available, which have a separate filter to remove the pulp and pips from your smoothies.

Visit a few department stores to see what is on offer and find a machine to suit your budget, your kitchen, and your lifestyle. With juicers, the prices range from the affordable to the astronomical: basic models start at around $40, where-as state-of-the-art masticating juicers can cost up to $3,000 for really efficient machines.

There are two types of juicer, and, as in all things, you get what you pay for. Centrifugal juicers work by finely chopping or grating the produce and spinning it round so that centrifugal force pushes it through a fine wire mesh, separating the juice from the pulp. They range in price from about $50 to $250 and although purists believe that they do not produce as many nutrients as their more efficient big brothers, the masticating juicers, they are excellent machines for part-time juicers.

Masticating juicers are more substantial machines that pulverize the fruit and vegetables by pushing it through a wire mesh with great force to separate the juice from the pulp. They extract larger amounts of juice than centrifugal juicers and therefore more nutrients. They are generally larger machines, more durable and hard-wearing, and naturally cost more. Prices start at about $200.

Juicing enthusiasts believe that centrifugal juicers instantly expose the juice to oxidization, which makes it deteriorate, so it must be drunk immediately in order to gain real benefit. Masticating juicers, on the other hand, have slower rotating cutters that incorporate less oxygen, so juice from these machines will last for 24 hours if stored in a refrigerator. In fact, juice from any source will probably last for a day if stored in a sealed container in a fridge at a temperature between 35–38°F (2–4°C), just above freezing.

Another important consideration when choosing a juicer is how easily it dismantles. Thorough cleaning is vital both to preserve the juicer and to prevent the build-up of bacteria. Juice pulp gets stuck in every nook and cranny of the machine, so it must be taken apart, soaked, and scrubbed in hot soapy water after every juicing session. Try to examine the machine properly before you buy it to check how easy it is to take apart and reassemble. Nothing is more likely to put you off juicing than the prospect of a tedious washing-up session after each drink! A solution of white wine vinegar and water (mixed in a ratio of one to two) will soak away the stains of the more colorful produce.

Useful gadgets

Scales to weigh the produce – Chapter Two contains a rough guide to the

amount of juice you can expect to extract from unprepared fruit and vegetables.

Scrubbing brushes – one to scrub fruit and vegetables before juicing, and a smaller version, perhaps a toothbrush for cleaning awkward corners of the juicer. A bottle brush is also useful for those hard-to-reach corners.

Vegetable peeler – some produce should be peeled before juicing, particularly non-organic items, so make sure you have an efficient and comfortable-to-use peeler.

Chopping board – some fruit and vegetables will have to be chopped up in order to fit them into the juicer's feeder tube. It is sensible to keep one chopping board solely for the preparation of fruit and vegetables. If you have a garden and a compost heap, keep all the waste matter in something like an old ice cream tub to recycle in your garden. Similarly, the pulp from the juicer makes an excellent addition to a compost heap, providing an instant organic mush.

Two knives – a sharp fruit knife and a larger knife for tackling bigger items such as melons and pineapples.

Graters and choppers Graters are useful for citrus rinds or spices such as nutmeg. Specialist fruit and vegetable choppers (illustrated below) can also speed up the business of producing items small enough to fit into the juicer's feed tube. They work best on hard fruits such as apples or pears.

Measuring jug – make sure it has measurements in milliliters and fluid ounces to help you mix the juices correctly. It is sensible to juice each item separately and then to mix them in the measuring jug to ensure that the proportions for each recipe are correct.

Swizzle sticks – once the ingredients

are juiced, combine them in a glass or jug. A long-handled spoon will do just as well, but swizzle sticks are often brightly colored and add a sense of occasion.

Glasses – tall glasses are best. Make sure they are scrupulously clean so that the fantastic colors of the fresh juices and smoothies shine out.

Pineapple corer – If you are fond of pineapple, a pineapple coring gadget will be invaluable. It uses a corkscrew action to remove the tough center part and enables the extraction of the flesh as rings, leaving the shell intact. Why not make a tropical juice cocktail and drink it from the shell?

Back to basics

The king and queen of the juice world are carrots and apples. Both produce pleasant juices, delightful on their own, but also subtle enough to be mixed with any other fruit or vegetable that you may choose. Together, they make a great combination, and it is worth experimenting to find the perfect apple/carrot mix to suit your palate.

Some nutritionists believe that carrot juice should form the basis of all vegetable juice blends, and there is a great deal of sense in this advice. Carrots yield a reasonably large amount of juice and their comparatively sweet taste complements and, where necessary, masks the strong, savory, or earthy flavors of many other vegetables. For example, the juices of broccoli or dark green leafy vegetables should be diluted in a ratio of one to four – that's four times as much carrot juice – in order to make them more palatable.

Milks and yogurts

There are no hard and fast rules as to what exactly constitutes a smoothie, but they may contain milk, yogurt, or ice cream, to give a delicious thick consistency. Drinks like this have been made for generations in Asia and the Indian subcontinent: lassis are fantastic fresh yogurt-based drinks which provide an excellent counterpoint to the region's highly flavored dishes. They can be spicy or sweet, but essentially any fresh produce can be blended with yogurt

Milk forms an important part of a balanced diet, and it has been estimated that milk and dairy products provide about 55% of the calcium consumed every day. Apart from the really important nutrients (see page 8), milk also contains butyric acid and conjugated linoleic acid, compounds that scientists believe are anti-carcinogens.

Yogurt is produced by fermenting milk with the addition of a starter culture of *streptococcus thermophillus* and *lactobacillus bulgaricus*. While yogurt contains many of the same benefits as milk, it can be suitable for those who are lactose-intolerant, because the live cultures break down the lactose in the milk during fermentation, converting it to lactic acid. (Lactose is the sugar present in milk.) The enzymes within the lactic acid in yogurt encourage the growth of healthy bacteria in the gut, raising levels of vitamin B and improving digestion. Goats milk yogurt is good for skin problems

Plain yogurt is an excellent source of calcium, soothes irritated stomachs, and like milk, promotes bone development. It is often prescribed for patients under going drug treatment as it restores the natural bacteria in the gut which can be destroyed by antibiotics.

Dairy alternatives

For those who suffer from a lactose intolerance, soy milk is an excellent substitute, or they may consider making your own nut 'milk'. Soy milk is rich in protein, while being low in saturated fats.

It contains calcium and the phyto-nutrients, in particular genistein, which tackle cancer (especially breast, ovarian and prostate cancer). Soy milk is manufactured by soaking soy beans in water, then straining them to remove the fiber. It can be purchased in most supermarkets or health food stores and is also available as yogurt.

Coconut milk adds a touch of Caribbean flavor to smoothie or juice recipes. It is available commercially, or you can simply bang a hole in a coconut, pour the milk out and eat the flesh or save it for cooking.

Certain nuts such as sunflower seeds, almonds, cashews or sesame seeds, can be blanched or soaked, and blended with water to produce delicious, intensely flavored 'milk'. The liquid is high in both protein and calories. The less water you use, the thicker the consistency of the resulting milk, but it should be strained before use. As a rule of thumb, use three- to four times more water than nuts; so for one cup of nuts, use three or four cups of water. Nut milk can be kept in the fridge for a few days, although it will begin to separate, so must be stirred before use. Made fresh, it is easy to blend in berries, bananas or anything else you fancy for a richly flavored smoothie.

Almond milk recipe

4 oz blanched almonds
1 tablespoon honey (optional)
8 fl oz water and four ice cubes

Add the honey and almonds to a blender with the ice cubes and ice. Whiz until the mixture is a paste and then gradually add the water until the mixture is smooth. You can drink it as is, or mix it with your favorite fruit as a smoothie.

Is it fresh?

Avocados: Cup your hands around the fruit and squeeze gently. If it gives slightly it is ready to eat. Pressing with your fingertips will cause bruising. Under-ripe avocados can be ripened at home (see box below).

Bananas: Green bananas will ripen in a few days at room temperature; however, they bruise easily – this is seen as brown flecks on the skin.

Blackberries: These should be plump and glossy with a purple color. If hulls are still attached, the berries could have been picked while under-ripe and may lack flavor.

Cabbage: Check the heart of the vegetable is firm by pressing the center with your thumb. Avoid specimens with discolored outer leaves or damaged patches.

Cauliflower: Always pull back the outer leaves to check for insects between the florets. The florets should be firm and white.

Citrus fruits should feel heavy for their size.

Cucumbers: select cucumbers that are firm with shiny skins.

Grapes: Shake a bunch of grapes before buying them, if any fall off they aren't fresh.

Lettuce: Choose lettuces that are firm and crisp. Avoid those with yellowing outer leaves.

Melons: Hold the melon firmly with both hands and lightly press the area around the tip of the melon, which is opposite to the stem end. It should give slightly.

Peppers: Should have a firm and shiny outer skin. Like apples, they wrinkle when dehydrated and aging.

Pineapple: To check for ripeness in a pineapple, pull a leaf at the top of the fruit bulb. If it pulls out easily the fruit is ripe.

Ripening fruit and vegetables

All fruit and vegetables give off a chemical – a plant hormone called ethylene – as they mature. Some plants still produce this chemical after being harvested, but not all. Apples, bananas and tomatoes are particularly excretory. This can be to your advantage: to ripen unripe fruit, put it in a bag with an apple or a ripe tomato and keep in a warm, dark place until the fruit is ripe.

How to choose decent produce

When you begin juicing, simply buy a selection of ingredients that you like. Once you are more experienced, broaden your selection. One of the best ways to select really fresh produce is to sniff it. Many fruits, such as mangoes and melons have a faintly floral aroma when ripe that disappears as the fruit ages. Citrus fruits should always feel heavy for their size – this is a sign that they are really juicy. Lighter specimens are likely to be shrivelling and dehydrating with age. Melons and pears should be gently pressed at the stalk end, and should give slightly if they are ripe. Kiwi fruit should also give a little when squeezed gently. Apples and pears should be smooth, berries should be firm and not mushy, while grapes should retain a slight 'bloom' on their skins.

Citrus fruits are probably best for the novice juicer: they are familiar, easy to store, and are satisfyingly juicy.

Storage

Most citrus fruits will produce more juice if stored at room temperature. If they have been kept in the fridge, warm in a microwave on high power for about five seconds.

Citrus or hard fruits can be stored for longer than a week and still retain much of their goodness. Wash and dry the fruit and wrap each item in newspaper. Pack in a plastic bag or place in a box and store in a cool dry place.

Soft berries should be examined on a tray lined with paper towel and any damaged or moldy ones discarded. Cover with more paper towels before freezing.

How much juice?

As with all changes to your diet, do nothing suddenly. Having tried the recipes, you may want to embrace the juicing lifestyle with the zeal of a convert, but make sure you enjoy juices as part of a balanced diet. Juicing removes the fiber from fruit and vegetables and cannot permanently fulfil the complete nutritional needs of the body. Everyone needs a balance of fats, carbohydrates, and proteins to function properly. Try to drink equal amounts of vegetable juice and fruit juice in order to avoid consuming too much sugar (which is present as fructose in all fruit).

It is really very hard to overdose on juices, but remember the adage, 'moderation in all things' and begin gradually, limiting yourself to two glasses of juice a day. Nutritionists advise novice juicers to drink no more than three 8 fl oz (225 ml) glasses of fresh

Don't neglect vegetable juices – they contain less sugar and a wide variety of nutrients.

juice a day. If your children seem enthusiastic, by all means let them help, but limit their intake to 5 fl oz (150 ml) a day, perhaps by letting them sample different blends in small 'shot' glasses, or by diluting their juices with water. The body must grow accustomed to digesting the concentrated nutrients released by fresh juices. A glass of fresh juice is the best multivitamin supplement of all, and is much tastier than the average tablet!

Once you are used to the effects of juice on your body you may want to try a juice detox plan over the course of a day or two. This will flush out your system, remove impurities, and thoroughly revitalize you – although this is something for adults only. Many books on juicing include a detoxification diet, a program designed to clean out your digestive system and revitalize your general well-being. This book contains a one-day detox plan, but it is not advisable to undertake such a diet if you are in poor health or if you are on medication – if in doubt consult your doctor.

Some people have adopted juicing after being diagnosed with a serious illness, but most ardent converts often use juicing in conjunction with conventional medicine. Juicing can help improve your overall health and will strengthen the body to fight disease, but it is unlikely to eliminate serious symptoms. Fresh juices are the best way to increase your intake of essential vitamins and minerals and may well alleviate minor conditions or allergies.

Tips

In hot weather, use frozen berries straight from the freezer to chill your juices. If you crave a berry drink in winter, you will find packs of frozen berries in most supermarkets.

Dilute dark green vegetable juices such as spinach or broccoli, or dark red vegetable juices, such as beetroot, in a ratio of four parts mixer to one part green juice. They are not only strong, but their flavor is an acquired taste. Carrot or apple are the best juices to balance the flavors, but cucumber is also useful.

Fruit and vegetable juices generally do not mix well and may cause flatulence. The exceptions are carrot and apple, which can be mixed with virtually anything else.

DON'T make large quantities – fresh juice oxidizes (and may turn an off-putting brown color) quickly. If you have any left over, refrigerate immediately.

DON'T gulp your juice, however delicious. Sip it slowly, savoring and absorbing the flavors and allowing it to mix with the enzymes in your saliva.

DO drink both fruit and vegetable juices – too many fruit juices will fill you up with fructose (fruit sugars) and vegetable mixes contain many vital vitamins not present in fruits.

DO make something suitable for the time of day – fresh fruit is perfect for breakfast, whereas Brussels sprouts are not, in general, such a pleasant start to the day.

DO experiment – use the recipes in this book as a basis for your own concoctions.

The most important thing is just to enjoy the great taste and myriad flavors of fresh juices. You can sit back sure in the knowledge that these delicious drinks are actually doing you good!

The Goodness in Greens. . . and Reds, Oranges and Yellows

This chapter deals with a wide variety of fruit and vegetables, explaining their properties, the vitamins and minerals they contain, and the potential health benefits to be had by including them in your diet. It is also worth noting how the vitamins and minerals work on the body. The recipes in the following chapters are based on this information and it will help you to create your own recipes to target certain areas of your health that need improving. The data sections are really only an approximate guide to the amount of juice you can expect from different fruit and vegetables; yield depends on the juicer and the size and quality of the fruit used.

Fruit

Bursting with natural goodness, fruits are made up of between 75 percent and 90 percent water, so they will naturally quench your thirst as well as pumping you full of energy. They can be classified in four main categories, all of which can be mixed together for the purpose of juicing. For maximum flavor, it is best to eat whatever is in season, especially if you use organic fruit. Fruit that has travelled hundreds, or even thousands, of miles to your supermarket may well look delicious, but ask yourself how long it has taken to reach you, and how many preservatives have been used to sustain it. Many fruits are picked while still a little under-ripe and are only allowed to fully ripen once at their final warehouse destination. Local, seasonal fruit will nearly always taste better and will be cheaper than those items whose airfare you have paid for.

Pome Fruits
Apples

Packed into millions of lunch boxes every day, apples are probably the most popular fruit of all. There are over 7,000 varieties, but the best juice is probably made with Cox's Orange Pippins or Russets. Choose apples with firm, undamaged skin. Smell them and inhale a fresh 'appley' aroma. Do not select those with waxy skins, as this often hides a woolly, flavorless fruit. They can be juiced whole (if the juicer feed tube allows), but it is probably better to chop them into quarters. They do not need to be peeled or cored, but must be washed thoroughly. Apple seeds are a valuable source of potassium, so do not bother removing the pits. Generally, the greener an apple's skin, the sharper or more tart its juice will taste.

Juicing data

Best for: pectin and vitamin C, which lower cholesterol.

Calories: 52 kilocalories/3.5 oz (100 g).

Number needed to make 3.5 fl oz (100 ml): two.

Preparation: wash, chop to fit feed tube. No need to peel or core.

Pears

Pears have similar attributes to apples, and pear juice, like apple juice, is endlessly versatile. Although there are over 5,000 varieties to choose from, only twelve or so are readily available in the shops. Choose perfect fruit, as pears deteriorate very quickly once picked to become woolly or soft. The stem end should 'give' slightly when gently pressed between your thumb and forefinger.

Rich in betacarotene, folic acid and vitamin C, pears also harbour small amounts of vitamins B1, B2, B3, B5, and B6. The juice oxidizes and turns brown very fast, so drink it as soon as it is made.

Juicing data

Best for: potassium. Pears cause a gradual rise in blood sugar so they are excellent for diabetics.

Calories: 60 kilocalories/3.5 oz (100 g).

Number needed to make 3.5 fl oz (100 ml): two.

Preparation: wash, chop to fit feed tube. No need to peel or core.

Apple Juice

Apples contain vitamins A and C and are high in pectin, the soluble dietary fiber, which makes the juice cloudy; apples are an excellent antidote to digestive troubles. It is the most versatile fruit juice, mild and sweet enough to be mixed with virtually any other fruit or vegetable juice, yet delicious on its own.

Stone fruits

Apricots

Known to the Romans and Greeks as 'golden eggs of the sun,' apricots are small orange/pinky fruits with a subtle flavor. They originally grew wild in China, migrated to Persia and Armenia, and were probably introduced to southern Europe by the troops of Alexander the Great in the 3rd century BC. Once picked they do not travel well, so find firm fruit with intense color and a smooth, perfumed skin. Full of betacarotene, vitamin C and minerals such as calcium and magnesium, apricots are terrific antioxidant cleansers and excellent for respiratory problems. They are not one of the juiciest fruits, so you will need several to produce a reasonable amount of juice and may want to mix it with another juice, or dilute it with water. Although the stone is edible and the kernel is used to flavor liqueurs such as Amaretto, it is not advisable to plunge it into your juicer.

Juicing data

Best for: vitamin A/betacarotene to increase immunity against illness and provide healthy skin, hair, teeth, and bones.

Calories: 28 kilocalories/3.5 oz (100 g).

Number needed to make 3.5 fl oz (100 ml): six.

Preparation: wash, remove stone and chop to fit feed tube. No need to remove skin.

Avocado

Like bananas, avocados are not really suitable for juicing, but are so full of goodness that is worth mashing one to mix with another juice (try carrot, tomato, or cucumber), or adding juice and avocado to a blender to make a veggie smoothie.

Avocados are high in vitamin E, which helps combat cardiovascular disease and boosts the immune system. It is also good for the skin as it triggers the body to produce more collagen, which helps prevent wrinkles.

Juicing data

Best for: potassium, which helps combat fatigue, poor complexion, and depression.

Calories: 223 kilocalories/3.5 oz (100 g).

Number needed to make 3.5 fl oz (100 ml): n/a.

Preparation: cut in half, remove stone and scoop flesh into blender to mix with other juices, or mash with a fork and stir into another juice.

Cherries

There are hundreds of varieties of cherry, falling into three main categories – sweet, sour, and hybrid. Sweet cherries are obviously most suitable for juicing and, although rather fiddly to prepare, the delicious red juice is worth the effort. Cherries are rich in vitamin B2 (riboflavin), betacarotene, and folic acid, so are excellent for healthy eyes, skin, and hair.

Juicing data

Best for: vitamin B2 (riboflavin) to promote release of energy.

Calories: 47 kilocalories/3.5 oz (100 g).

Amount needed to make 3.5 fl oz (100 ml): 5–7 oz (150–200 g).

Preparation: wash and cut in half to remove the stones. No need to peel.

Nectarines

Once known as 'Persian plums', nectarines are close cousins of peaches. In reality they are a smooth-skinned variety of peach, and originated in China. Whether it is the slightly more acidic flavor or the absence of velvety downy skin, nectarines lack the luxurious flavor and aroma inherent in peaches, but they are nevertheless, delicious fruit. Choose unblemished fruit that is bright, firm and smooth. They contain slightly more minerals – potassium and phosphorus – and, like peaches, are rich in betacarotene, folic acid and vitamin C.

Juicing data

Best for: potassium and phosphorus to preserve the nervous system

Calories: 45 kilocalories/3.5 oz (100 g).

Number needed to make 3.5 fl oz (100 ml): two.

Preparation: wash, remove stone and chop to fit feed tube. No need to remove skin.

Peaches

Velvety, juicy, and voluptuous, ripe peaches are always a treat and have been prized throughout history. They have been called the "nectar of the gods" and the French found them so irresistible that they christened one variety *têton de Venus* – "Venus's breasts". They have a sweet, floral aroma and sweet juice that is tart enough not to be cloying. Peaches do not ripen after they have been picked, so select fruit that are firm, but slightly yielding when squeezed gently. They soften slightly when kept at room temperature, but if left too long the skin will wrinkle and the flesh will become woolly – a huge disappointment.

Peaches contain carotenes (which is present in their yellow flesh), flavonoids, folic acid, and vitamin C. Their gentle flavors make them good for irritated stomachs and the antioxidants help protect against cancer and heart disease.

Juicing data

Best for: flavonoids to protect against degenerative disease.

Calories: 60 kilocalories/3.5 oz (100 g).

Number needed to make 3.5 fl oz (100 ml): two.

Preparation: wash, remove stone and chop to fit feed tube. No need to remove skin.

Plums

Plums are smooth-skinned and range in color from yellow through crimson to deep purple. There are three main types, which grow all over the world – European, Japanese, and west Asian – so there is usually one variety in season. Plums have a sweet, juicy flesh with a degree of acidity, which makes them excellent for juicing. Choose plums that are firm but yield slightly when pressed; they ripen fast and will keep for a couple of days at room temperature, longer if stored in a fridge. They are rich in folic acid, vitamin C and betacarotene, and incorporate a range of minerals.

Juicing data

Best for: betacarotene to build up immunity against disease.

Calories: 38 kilocalories/3.5 oz (100 g).

Number needed to make 3.5 fl oz (100 ml): four to six, depending on size.

Preparation: wash, remove stone, and chop to fit feed tube. No need to remove skin.

Berries

Blackberries

Like raspberries, blackberries are members of the rose family and grow on thorny upright bushes. The ancient Greeks prized them for their medicinal properties and they are rich in dietary fiber, betacarotenes, and vitamins C and E. An ideal mixing juice, blackberries contain many ingredients to fight the free radicals that age our bodies.

Blackberries are at their most prolific from the end of August into September; do not pick them after September as they will have lost their flavor and become acid. One folk legend reinforces this by mentioning that the Devil infects them after September and makes them foul. They do not keep well, but, like raspberries, can be frozen on baking sheets and then packed in bags or containers for later use.

Juicing data

Best for: calcium to preserve teeth and bones.

Calories: 30 kilocalories/3.5 oz (100 g).

Amount needed to make 3.5 fl oz (100 ml): 7 oz (200 g).

Preparation: wash carefully and use immediately.

Blackcurrants

Blackcurrants are juicy, acidic berries that make a strongly flavored juice rich in vitamin C, and are best mixed with apple juice. It was only in the 16th century that they became valued as health-giving fruit, but since then they have been used to treat colds and throat infections. Pigments in the skin contain bacterial and anti-inflammatory qualities, so folk remedies are once again reinforced by scientific fact.

Blackcurrants remain fresh if stored in a fridge for a few days and also freeze well. They need minimal preparation – simply strip them from the twigs, rinse, and juice!

Juicing data

Best for: vitamin C and iron, act as antioxidant to protect against degenerative disease.

Calories: 28 kilocalories/3.5 oz (100 g).

Amount needed to make 3.5 fl oz (100 ml): 5 oz (150 g).

Preparation: strip currants from stalks and wash.

Cranberries

In recent years cranberries have acquired something of a reputation as the best treatment for urinary infections such as cystitis, but they have a long history as berries with protective properties. Waxy-skinned cranberries remain fresh for a long time, and during the 17th and 18th centuries sailors stored large quantities on board their ships so that they could be consumed during their voyages to protect against scurvy. They grow wild in both northern Europe and North America, but the Pilgrim Fathers discovered that the American varieties were larger and juicier than those from home, and they became a staple part of their diet. (This was the first recorded instance of the British being won over by the impressive size and quality of American produce...)

Containing a potent cocktail of vitamins C and D, along with potassium and carotene, cranberry juice helps to prevent *E. coli* bacteria attaching itself to the walls of the urinary tract, hence its use in treating urinary infections.

Choose plump, bright red fruit. Fresh cranberries will keep for several weeks in the fridge. A naturally tart juice, it mixes well with orange or apple juice.

Juicing data

Best for: iodine, which acts as a cleanser.

Calories: 15 kilocalories/3.5 oz (100 g).

Amount needed to make 3.5 fl oz (100 ml): 7 oz (200 g).

Preparation: wash.

Raspberries

The deep red color of raspberries is somehow reflected in their flavor and aroma. Cultivated since the Middle Ages, they grow wild in cool, damp environments, such as northern Europe, Alaska, and Asia. All berries contain the phytonutrient ellagic acid, a powerful antioxidant, which has demonstrated anti-cancer properties in experiments. Raspberries are also rich in magnesium, and can help regulate the menstrual cycle and relieve the symptoms of pre-menstrual syndrome. Indeed, raspberry leaf tea has long been advocated to ease labor pains.

Raspberries freeze well (unlike strawberries, which collapse) if they are placed in a single layer on a baking sheet, frozen, and then stored in bags. It is worth gathering extra in the summer for a winter treat. There is no need to defrost them before juicing.

Juicing data

Best for: zinc, vital for many of the body's regenerative processes, and to maintain acid/alkaline balance within body.

Calories: 25 kilocalories/3.5 oz (100 g).

Amount needed to make 3.5 fl oz (100 ml): 7 oz (200 g).

Preparation: wipe with a damp cloth if dirty, or wash carefully before hulling them. Do not wash once the green tops have been removed, as they will become waterlogged.

Strawberries

"Doubtless God could have made a better berry, but doubtless he never did," wrote an anonymous writer in the 16th century. With their jewel-like color and delectable flavor, strawberries have always been among the world's favorite fruit. Their short season makes them especially sought-after, so they are always a treat. They are cultivated more widely today, so are available out of season, but well-travelled, chilled, strawberries somehow lack the intense flavor of locally-grown berries.

Strawberry juice is not only a beautiful, vivid pink color, but it also contains plenty of vitamins B and C, and is rich in potassium and magnesium. It is an excellent cleansing juice, and will help restore your body's mineral balance. Actually, the delicious flavor alone is enough to perk you up and give you extra energy!

Juicing data

Best for: vitamin C.

Calories: 30 kilocalories/3.5 oz (100 g).

Amount needed to make 3.5 fl oz (100 ml): 7 oz (200 g).

Preparation: wipe with a damp cloth, if dirty, or wash carefully before hulling them. Do not wash once the green tops have been removed, as they will become waterlogged.

Citrus fruits

Citrus fruits were almost made for juicing, being tangy, brightly colored, and extremely juicy. Their bitter peel – far too bitter to juice – contains intensely scented aromatic oil that fills the kitchen with a summery, floral smell.

Lemons

With their distinctive shape and sharp taste, lemons have been used for centuries to cleanse palates and enliven food. Lemons originated in India or Malaysia, were introduced to Assyria, where the soldiers of Alexander the Great discovered them. They took them home to Greece where they were used in medicinal and cosmetic compounds. In the 12th and 13th centuries, they were transported to mainland Europe by the Crusaders, and by the 17th and 18th centuries they were grown under glass, and provided vital protection for sailors in the fight against scurvy.

Lemon Juice

The heady aroma of lemons and the intense scent of the zest are far more pleasurable sensory experiences than the acid taste of neat lemon juice. Mixed with other juices, however, lemon juice adds "bite" to many juice cocktails.

Lemons are rich in vitamin C – they contain twice as much as oranges – and their juice is extremely strong, so should always be diluted. Although the peel contains intense aromatic oils, it should always be removed before juicing, partly because many lemons are waxed to prolong their shelf life, which ruins the flavor of the juice.

Lemons become paler as they age, so select deep yellow fruit that feel heavy for their size. Before juicing, roll the fruit between the palms of your hands to loosen the flesh. Remove the skin, but leave as much pith as possible as it is full of flavonoids.

Juicing data

Best for: vitamin C.

Calories: 22 kilocalories/3.5 oz (100 g).

Number needed to make 3.5 fl oz (100 ml): three.

Preparation: peel and quarter.

Oranges

Like all citrus juices, oranges are full of fruit sugars, which provide an extra burst of energy at the start of the day. They originated in China and gradually spread to Europe, carried by traders and soldiers. During the Middle Ages, they were highly desirable, and regarded as a luxury item available only to the very rich. By the 17th century, with the establishment of regular trade routes to India, oranges became more widely available, and were sold throughout Europe.

There are two groups of oranges – sweet and bitter. Bitter oranges cannot be eaten raw and are used in preserves, such as marmalade, or liqueurs such as Grand Marnier. Sweet oranges are available all year round. They are full of goodness, with twice the adult daily allowance of vitamin C. Juicing (rather than simply squeezing) adds more goodness to the drink, as the pith is juiced along with the flesh and contains bioflavonoids, which help the body absorb vitamin C. The seeds are also a potent source of calcium, magnesium, and potassium, so once the orange skin is removed, use the rest of

Orange Juice

The classic breakfast drink, freshly squeezed orange juice is a brilliant start to the day. The tangy aroma is refreshing and comforting, and the wonderful flavor both reviving and energizing. Fresh OJ is a drink for all seasons and any time of the day.

the fruit with equanimity and enjoy a frothy, almost creamy juice.

Juicing data

Best for: vitamin C.

Calories: 46 kilocalories/3.5 oz (100 g).

Number needed to make 3.5 fl oz (100 ml): two.

Preparation: peel and quarter.

Grapefruit

Grapefruit are the largest variety of citrus fruits at 4–7 inches (10–18 cm) in diameter, and their flesh ranges in color from pale yellow to rosy pink. Generally, the pinker the flesh, the sweeter the fruit. They produce a reviving fresh juice that is far less acidic than lemon juice, yet less sweet than orange juice. One grapefruit incorporates more than one and a half times the daily vitamin C allowance, as well as potassium and pectin, which is recommended for those suffering from circulatory or digestive problems.

Juicing data

Best for: pectin, to improve circulatory problems.

Calories: 32 kilocalories/3.5 oz (100 g).

Number needed to make 3.5 fl oz (100 ml): one.

Preparation: peel and break into segments to fit the feeder tube.

Limes

Emerald green and the smallest citrus fruit, limes have thin skins and a refreshing, acidic juice. They are grown in tropical regions from Egypt to the West Indies, but, despite many attempts, have failed to thrive in Mediterranean areas. Lime juice was the original cure for scurvy, the degenerative disease caused by lack of vitamin C, which plagued sailors in the 17th and 18th centuries.

They are the most perishable of all citrus fruit, so choose unblemished, heavy fruit. Lime juice, fizzy water and crushed ice make a spectacularly cool drink on a hot day, and lime juice also mixes well with melon juice.

Juicing data

Best for: vitamin C.

Calories: 20 kilocalories/3.5 oz (100 g).

Number needed to make 3.5 fl oz (100 ml): three.

Preparation: peel and break into segments to fit the feeder tube.

Mandarins

Also known as tangerines, clementines or satsumas, these easy-peeling, small orange fruit originated in China and arrived in Europe during Roman times, carried by Arab traders. In Britain they are inextricably linked with childhood memories of Christmas, as it is traditional to find a tangerine in the toe of the stocking-full of presents left by Father Christmas. The pale orange-colored juice is less tart than freshly squeezed orange juice and easier on the digestion.

Juicing data

Best for: vitamin B1 (thiamine) to break down carbohydrates and assist in energy production. Especially useful for smokers and those taking the oral contraceptive pill who often suffer from a B1 deficiency.

Calories: 35 kilocalories/3.5 oz (100 g).

Number needed to make 3.5 fl oz (100 ml): three.

Preparation: peel and break into segments to fit the feeder tube.

Exotic fruits
Bananas

Bananas do not juice well, but if you use soft specimens and then juice something juicy like melon, it will flush the banana through the juicer. However, it may be easier to use bananas in smoothies (see pages 187–202), as they can be blended more successfully. They provide such a great flavor that it is a shame to be a complete juicer puritan! Alternatively, mash up a banana and combine it with other juices.

Bananas are rich in potassium, a mineral vital to the functioning of body cells and vitamin B6, which balances the metabolism. They promote the release of serotonin, the body's natural "happy" chemical. They are a soothing food and beneficial to an upset digestive tract.

Juicing data

Best for: vitamin B6 (pyridoxine),which metabolizes protein, sugars, and fatty acids. Preserves nerves and skin.

Calories: 79 kilocalories/3.5 oz (100 g).

Number needed to make 3.5 fl oz (100 ml): n/a

Preparation: peel and mash with a fork, or add to liquidizer with other juices.

Kiwi fruit

The uninspiring furry skin of a kiwi fruit hides a beautiful green gem of a fruit that is rich in vitamins C and E, as well as potassium. Once known as "Chinese gooseberries "because they originated in the Yangtze valley, kiwis are now cultivated in New Zealand (hence the name), Australia, South America and South Africa.

Choose firm fruit with an unwrinkled skin; hard fruit will ripen at room temperature, but store away from other fruit, as hormones released by the kiwis will cause other fruits to ripen too fast. Kiwi produces a thick, bright green juice that is mild enough to drink alone, but tastes wonderful when mixed with fruits such as orange, pineapple, or melon.

Juicing data

Best for: potassium, for cell regeneration.

Calories: 61 kilocalories/3.5 oz (100 g).

Number needed to make 3.5 fl oz (100 ml): three.

Preparation: peel off the skin, and chop to fit the feeder tube.

Mango

Juicy, luxurious, tropical fruits, mangos are delicately scented smooth-skinned fruit with a sweet, irresistibly juicy flesh encasing a large stone. They are full of vitamin C and carotenes, which are helpful in controlling high blood pressure; they also provide an excellent boost to the immune system.

Juicing data

Best for: vitamin C and carotenes to boost the immune system.

Calories: 60 kilocalories/3.5 oz (100 g).

Number needed to make 3.5 fl oz (100 ml): half.

Preparation: cut into quarters, remove stone and scoop out the flesh from the skin.

Grapes and Melons

Grapes

Grapes are an excellent source of vitamin E, an antioxidant that combats the damaging, aging effects of free radicals on our bodies. The juice is either pale green or pale red (depending on the color of the grape skins) with a sweet, piquant flavor from the high fructose content.

Grapes are among the oldest cultivated fruits and were fermented by the Ancient Egyptians (if not earlier), but probably only for religious purposes, rather than for partying. They are highly nutritious, and in the 19th century a short-lived spa treatment was devised, the uvarium, with health-giving treatments based entirely on grapes. Red grape skins contain a substance called resveratrol, a naturally occurring phenol, which scientists have shown can inhibit cancer growth at several different stages, from the

initiation of DNA damage to transformation of the cell into cancer, and growth and spread of the tumor.

The perfect bunch of grapes should be of uniform size and color; they will last well if stored in the fridge, but remove them before juicing to get them to room temperature and allow the flavor to develop.

Juicing data

Best for: a phytochemical that protects cell DNA from damage.

Calories: 60 kilocalories/3.5 oz (100 g).

Amount needed to make 3.5 fl oz (100 ml): 5 oz (150 g).

Preparation: remove from stalks and rinse. No need to remove pips.

Melon

Orange or yellow-colored melons such as Cantaloupe, Galia, Honeydew or Charentais varieties produce refreshing juice that the digestive system can absorb very quickly. It is delicious mixed with tropical fruits such as bananas or pineapples, and softens the acidity of oranges. However, to maximize the body's absorption of the vitamins and minerals in melons, it should be drunk on its own. It contains betacarotene, folic acid, and minerals such as calcium, chlorine, and magnesium; and if combined with a little ginger, produces an excellent cure for queasiness.

They can be divided into two groups: summer fruits, such as Galias, have cross-hatched skin, while winter fruit have smooth or finely-ridged pale or bright yellow rind with pale flesh (like the Honeydew). Gently press the stalk end to discover whether it is ripe – it should "give" slightly. Ripe melons also have a wonderful "melony" aroma.

Watermelons have a very high water content and are fabulously refreshing. They produce a beautiful, dark pinky-brown juice if the pits are juiced too, even darker if the rind is used as well.

Juicing data

Best for (watermelons): vitamin B5 (pantothenic acid), which metabolizes energy. Yellow melons: folic acid, which preserves the nervous system and helps prevent spina bifida in developing foetuses.

Calories: 25 kilocalories/3.5 oz (100 g).

Number needed to make 3.5 fl oz (100 ml): one quarter (Galia/Charentais).

Preparation: cut into quarters, scrape the pits out if you wish, remove flesh from the rind in chunks, and juice.

Vegetables

Juicing vegetables seems slightly less fun than fruit, but, if you are committed to juicing, you should also consume vegetable juices, because they provide a very different selection of vitamins and minerals vital for good health. Some vegetable juice is very powerful, with strong flavors that are rather less palatable than most fruit juices. However, just about all vegetable juices can be successfully mixed with carrot juice, which is mild and sweet. As you grow accustomed to the taste of vegetable juice, you can alter the mix to decrease the mixer juice and increase the other ingredients.

Beetroot

Beetroot seems a particularly East European remedy, where it has been used to treat convalescents and to build up resistance to disease. It is also regarded as a powerful blood cleanser. Beetroot is rich in folates and folic acid, so it provides women thinking of becoming pregnant, or in the early stages of pregnancy, with efficient protection against spina bifida in the foetus. For everyone else, it produces a juice of spectacular purple color, with a taste as strong as its color. It is a useful cleanser and will help detoxify the kidneys, but should be taken in moderation. It is advisable to mix it with milder juices in the ratio of one part beetroot to four parts of something else.

Juicing data

Best for: folic acid, which preserves the nervous system and helps prevent spina bifida in developing foetuses.

Calories: 44 kilocalories/3.5 oz (100 g).

Number needed to make 3.5 fl oz (100 ml): half a smallish beetroot.

Preparation: cut the fibrous bottom off, scrub thoroughly, and chop up. There is no need to peel unless you want to.

Broccoli

A crucifer vegetable, broccoli incorporates many phytonutrients, which help fight cancer. It is also rich in iron, so is a useful restorative for the run-down, and contains a rich source of vitamin B5 (pantothenic acid), which makes energy available to the body. Broccoli juice is dark green and bitter, and should be diluted to make it more palatable.

Juicing data

Best for: magnesium, vital for the nervous system and brain function.

Calories: 28 kilocalories/3.5 oz (100 g).

Number needed to make 3.5 fl oz (100 ml): about eight small florets.

Preparation: cut off fibrous stalk ends and wash.

Brussels sprouts

Your mother was right when she said that sprouts were good for you: Brussels sprouts are the highest producer of folates, which produce white blood cells and improve the body's regenerative and restorative powers. They also contain impressive amounts of folic acid, vital for the healthy development of babies in the womb, as well as vitamin B6 (pyridoxine), which promotes an efficient metabolic process.

Cabbage Juice

Drunk neat, cabbage juice may seem like a gastronomic punishment, but it can improve digestive troubles and is made more palatable by mixing with sweeter flavors.

Juicing data

Best for: zinc, which regenerates cells and balances the acid/alkaline levels in the body.

Calories: 26 kilocalories/3.5 oz (100 g).

Number needed to make 3.5 fl oz (100 ml): about eight.

Preparation: remove outer layer of leaves and rinse.

Cabbage (red/white/Savoy)

Juice from the different varieties of cabbage is easily distinguishable, not least by its color: red cabbage juice is similar in color to beetroot, but has a slightly peppery flavor, while white cabbage produces a surprisingly sweet pale green juice. Cabbage juice is often prescribed

for digestive problems, especially stomach ulcers, and its taste can be improved if it is mixed with pineapple juice. It also contains plenty of iron and Savoy cabbages, in particular, are also full of chlorophyl, the green plant pigment, which helps restore red blood cell levels.

Juicing data

Best for: calcium, to promote healthy bones and teeth.

Calories: 22 (white); 25 (red) kilocalories/ 3.5 oz (100 g).

Amount needed to make 3.5 fl oz (100 ml): about a third of a small cabbage.

Preparation: rinse and chop to fit feeder tube.

Carrot

One carrot will supply enough betacarotene to fulfill a whole day's vitamin A requirement, and more importantly, the juice actually tastes good! Choose darker-colored carrots and simply scrub them and remove the tops and tails before juicing. Carrot juice is the sweetest of all vegetable juices and can be mixed with anything else to improve the taste of more strongly flavored juices.

Juicing data

Best for: betacarotene, an antioxidant that protects against degenerative disease.

Carrot Juice

One of the great staples of the juicing store cupboard, carrot juice is delicious alone, or can be mixed with virtually any other fruit or vegetable juice.

Calories: 35 kilocalories/3.5 oz (100 g).

Number needed to make 3.5 fl oz (100 ml): two.

Preparation: scrub, remove tops and tails; do not peel.

Celery

An old wives' tale claims that one actually burn more calories in eating a long stringy stalk of celery than one absorbs. Celery is undoubtedly low in calories and produces a slightly peppery-flavored juice, which mixes well with apple.

Juicing data

Best for: sodium, which helps maintain the correct fluid balance in the body.

Calories: 8 kilocalories/3.5 oz (100 g).

Number needed to make 3.5 fl oz (100 ml): two stalks.

Preparation: remove leafy ends and chop into chunks.

Cucumber

Cucumbers are full of water and produce a mild juice that is perfect for mixing with stronger flavors. Nevertheless, it is very refreshing by itself, and is full of minerals. It is an excellent diuretic, so would be an excellent detox ingredient.

Juicing data

Best for: potassium to aid cleansing.

Calories: 10 kilocalories/3.5 oz (100 g).

Number needed to make 3.5 fl oz (100 ml): half a large one.

Preparation: scrub and chop to fit the feeder tube.

Garlic

Garlic has long been used as a folk remedy: it prevents heart disease and has anti-carcinogenic qualities. It also has a pronounced and lingering flavor, so only one or two cloves are needed to flavor a drink. It contains the compound allicin, which is naturally antiviral, antifungal, and antibacterial, so it helps the body fight infections.

Juicing data

Best for: antiviral properties.

Calories: 117 kilocalories/3.5 oz (100 g).

Number needed to make 3.5 fl oz (100 ml): n/a.

Preparation: remove outer skin from clove.

Kale

A leafy green vegetable, kale is bursting with useful vitamins, minerals, and antioxidants. The juice is strong and should be diluted with four times as much carrot or apple juice. It is a good source of vitamin B1 (thiamine), B2 (riboflavin), and calcium; smokers and those on the oral contraceptive pill often suffer from a B1 deficiency.

Juicing data

Best for: vitamin B1 (thiamine) to break down carbohydrates and assist in energy production, Especially useful for smokers and those on the pill.

Calories: 53 kilocalories/3.5 oz (100 g).

Number needed to make 3.5 fl oz (100 ml): handful of leaves.

Preparation: rinse.

Leek

Leeks were prized by the ancient Egyptians, the Romans, and the Greeks for their health-giving properties. A member of the allium family – which also includes onions and garlic – the French traditionally used leeks to treat respiratory problems. They are rich in potassium, so are a useful diuretic. The pale green juice is a mild oniony flavor, useful for enlivening blander juices.

Juicing data

Best for: potassium, to aid detoxification and calcium to promote healthy bones.

Calories: 31 kilocalories/3.5 oz (100 g).

Number needed to make 3.5 fl oz (100 ml): one large leek.

Preparation: remove stalk, slice lengthways, rinse with water, and chop widthways into chunks.

Lettuce

Lettuce juice is surprisingly bitter, and varies from pale to dark green, depending on the variety of lettuce used. It is another strong juice and should be diluted with four parts of carrot or apple to one part lettuce.

Juicing data

Best for: betacarotene to supply the antioxidant vitamin A.

Calories: 11–18 kilocalories/3.5 oz (100 g).

Number needed to make 3.5 fl oz (100 ml): ten large leaves.

Preparation: rinse leaves.

Mange tout

Contains several B complex vitamins, (B1 and B2) and is a useful source of minerals. The body cannot manufacture minerals and must absorb them from food; they are vital to maintain the body's regenerative processes, and mange tout are a valuable source of calcium and magnesium. The juice is bright green and reasonably sweet, but may be improved if diluted.

Juicing data

Best for: magnesium, which helps brain function.

Calories: 42 kilocalories/3.5 oz (100 g).

Amount needed to make 3.5 fl oz (100 ml): 4 oz (125 g).

Preparation: rinse, then top and tail.

Onion

Onions have long been used in folk medicine as a cure for respiratory problems, urinary infections and as a general tonic or pick-me-up. Scientific trials have established that raw onions reduce blood clotting, and so protect the veins and arteries. Creamy and strong, the juice is probably best used as a mixer with milder flavors such as apple or carrot.

Juicing data

Best for: cholesterol-lowering properties.

Calories: 23 kilocalories/3.5 oz (100 g).

Number needed to make 3.5 fl oz (100 ml): two medium onions.

Preparation: remove outer skin, chop to fit feeder tube.

Parsley

A bright green juice that adds a delicate herby flavor. It is another strong juice, but the plant does not juice particularly well and it is often easier to finely chop it and scatter or stir it into your juice cocktail. It is a natural diuretic and is a useful cleansing juice.

Juicing data

Best for: iron, so excellent for the anaemic.

Calories: 43 kilocalories/3.5 oz (100 g).

Number needed to make 3.5 fl oz (100 ml): n/a.

Preparation: rinse.

Parsnip

Parsnips are always surprising in their sweetness, given their innocuous, bland color. They contain a number of B vitamins and are useful in improving the appearance of skin, hair, and nails.

Juicing data

Best for: folic acid, calcium, and magnesium.

Calories: 49 kilocalories/3.5 oz (100 g).

Number needed to make 3.5 fl oz (100 ml): two.

Preparation: remove stalks, scrub, and cut into chunks.

Pepper (capsicum)

Red capsicum peppers are sweeter than yellow or green ones (and hence slightly higher in calories), and red and yellow peppers contain four times as much vitamin C as oranges. Capsicum pepper juice is a great color and delicious mixed with tomato or carrot juice.

Juicing data

Best for: vitamin C.

Calories: 15–32 kilocalories/3.5 oz (100 g).

Number needed to make 3.5 fl oz (100 ml): three.

Preparation: rinse and chop to fit feeder tube.

Potato

Potato juice is definitely an acquired taste and needs to be mixed with something sweeter. However, it contains B vitamins, vitamin C, and betacarotene. It has been used by complementary therapists to treat both stomach ulcers and arthritis.

Juicing data

Best for: B vitamins and calcium.

Calories: 87 kilocalories/3.5 oz (100 g).

Number needed to make 3.5 fl oz (100 ml): three medium.

Preparation: scrub and chop into chunks; peel only if very muddy.

Spinach

Popeye's favorite! This is another strongly flavored juice that must be diluted with four parts mixer to one part spinach juice. Spinach will condition the entire digestive system. It contains large amounts of chlorophyl – an iron-containing compound. Iron is essential in delivering oxygen to all the body's cells; low iron levels lead to lethargy, and so iron-containing spinach aids restoration of energy levels particularly to those suffering from anaemia. Leafy green vegetables are always cited as providing excellent protection against cancer, and there is nothing leafier or greener than spinach!

Juicing data

Best for: potassium to regulate the body's water balance and regulate heart rhythm.

Calories: 25 kilocalories/3.5 oz (100 g).

Number needed to make 3.5 fl oz (100 ml): 20 large leaves.

Preparation: peel and break into segments to fit the feeder tube.

Tomato

Pink-orange color, very unlike cartons of commercially-prepared tomato juice. Delicious mixed with cucumber juice or by itself, tomatoes contain phytonutrients (specifically lycopene) that help protect against degenerative disease such as cancer. Scientific studies have shown that the consumption of ten or more tomatoes a week lowers men's susceptibility to prostate cancer by a third.

Juicing data

Best for: antioxidant lycopene, which protects joints, muscles and brain cells.

Calories: 14 kilocalories/3.5 oz (100 g).

Number needed to make 3.5 fl oz (100 ml): three.

Preparation: rinse and cut in half to fit feeder tube.

Wheatgrass

Wheatgrass is easy to grow at home from a packet of seeds available at health food stores. It is sometimes easier to juice it with carrots as the shoots are rather fine. The juice is bitter and foul, but has many health-giving properties, so mix 1–2 fl oz (25–50 ml) with apple or carrot for a palatable drink.

Juicing data

Best for: cleansing.

Calories: n/a

Number needed to make 1 fl oz (25 ml): a handful.

Preparation: add to juicer with carrots or apples.

Watercress

With a deep green color and a slightly peppery taste, watercress must be mixed with other juices in a ratio of one part watercress, four parts mixer. Watercress is a good source of iodine, which is beneficial to those with an underactive thyroid gland.

Juicing data

Best for: sulfur – essential to brain function; also promotes healthy skin and hair.

Calories: 14 kilocalories/3.5 oz (100 g).

Number needed to make 3.5 fl oz (100 ml): large handful.

Preparation: rinse and juice.

Energizing and Revitalizing Juices

Most people take up juicing encouraged by the great taste of fruit juices. However, if you want to absorb all the goodness available in fresh produce, it is sensible to take the plunge and start juicing vegetables too. Fruit juices are packed with the sugar fructose, which is an excellent energizer, so fruit juices are a terrific way to start the day, but, as the day wears on, most people rely on a slower release of energy. Vegetable juices contain the nutrients of the fiber and provide a greater balance of vitamins and minerals than would be obtained from fruit juices alone.

It is amazing how revitalizing just one glass of fresh juice can be. Incorporate fresh juice (and I don't mean from a carton!) into your breakfast routine and you will feel livelier, more energetic and able to confront most of what that the day has to offer. This is especially true if you wake up suffering from the effects of over-indulgence the night before – a fresh fruit juice mix is one of the best hangover cures possible. The nutrients in fresh juice will get to work on your pummelled liver, the vitamins and minerals will begin the process of restoring your metabolism to fitness, and it will rehydrate your dehydrated system.

Similarly, if at the end of the day you arrive home feeling over-wrought and exhausted, try a restorative cocktail of stress-busting B vitamins and minerals. Leafy green vegetables are a particularly important source of iron, which helps to combat the fatigue induced by stress.

Orange Dawn, see page 46

Instead of reaching for the gin bottle for a pre-dinner drink, get out the juicer and prepare an evening juice blend — you will feel healthier and very virtuous. Add crushed ice or a sprig of mint, and steer clear of overly sweet concoctions to cleanse your palate.

Worrying about energy levels and how to combat stress is a peculiarly modern preoccupation, not to say a luxury. Less privileged souls, many people in developing countries, for example, must concern themselves simply with finding their next meal – what it consists of is not something they can afford to be concerned with. Western society suffers from an over-abundance of choice, and a great many of us have chosen to clog up our systems with unhealthy food. We have come to expect cheap food and plenty of it.

Remember that you don't have to become a born-again juicer, eschewing all cooked food and fast food treats, to reap the benefit of fresh juice. Simply incorporating fresh juice into your diet is an excellent way to improve your overall health. What's more, it is a really delicious improvement to any diet!

All recipes make approximately 9 fl oz (250 ml) of juice. Juice each fruit separately and mix in a jug or glass with a spoon or swizzle stick. For tips on how to prepare the fruit and vegetables, see chapter two. Some of the reviving juices, perfect to sip at the end of the day, might benefit from being blended with ice, to make a slushy, cool drink. Many recipes require only half a pineapple or melon — preserve the remaining half of the fruit by storing it in the fridge, where it will be fine for a day or so.

Juicing in its most basic form.

Juices are identified as follows:

Wake-up!

The sun-kissed energy inherent in citrus fruit is a great way to start the day, but the rather acid effect on the stomach can be balanced by the milder flavors of melon or pineapple. Vegetable juices are generally not such a pleasant addition to a breakfast menu and can be saved for later in the day.

Revivers

Instead of reaching for the coffee and chocolate cookies in the middle of the day, try one of these recipes. Some could be made in the morning and taken to work in a vacuum flask – as long as the juice is kept cold, it will still taste fine at lunchtime. If you are at home, try a couple of these blender recipes with a banana, which is an ideal energy booster. Juice the other ingredients in the usual way, then add the whole lot to a blender with a banana for a thick, fruity treat.

If you find that you skip meals, a hearty juice is just the thing to replace lost energy and is far better than filling up on junk food or sweets.

Stress-beaters

The very act of slamming some fruit and veg into a juicer and watching the machine violently pulp the produce may reflect what you'd really like to do after a bad day, and may in itself be quite cathartic. Everyone experiences stress at some time, whether it is induced by pressure at work, the demands of coping with a young family, or, in many cases, both. The important thing is to recover some time for yourself, so if you can banish everyone and find fifteen minutes to concoct and enjoy a delicious juice, you will quickly recover your equilibrium.

Fatigue zappers

When you're feeling exhausted, the last thing you want to do is get out the juicer, but make the effort and you may be surprised by the results. Leafy green vegetables are especially good to restore lost energy levels, as they are high in iron. Many people feel particularly tired at the end of the day because their blood sugar is low after a day of snatched snacks and skipped meals. A glass of juice will not only restore your energy levels, but will also help to line your stomach and fill you up.

Vital ingredients:
iron

Best juices:
raspberry, peach, strawberry, kiwi fruit

Best vegetables:
spinach, broccoli, watercress

Insomnia cures

Bananas contain the amino acid tryptophan, which manufactures serotonin, the neurotransmitter, which governs sleep patterns. Low levels of serotonin often result in inadequate sleep patterns. Carbohydrates help the body absorb tryptophan, so try theses juices with a slice of toast before bed. The blended banana has a lovely texture, which is relaxing in itself.

"It is said that the effect of eating too much lettuce is 'soporific'." Readers who can recall the tales of Beatrix Potter will remember the cautionary tale of the Flopsy Bunnies, who fell asleep on Mr McGregor's pile of grass clippings after a heavy lunch of lettuces. Lettuces contain calcium, magnesium, and vitamins B3 and B6, all of which soothe the nervous system and help relax the body. If you prefer something savory before you sleep, try a combination of lettuce and carrot juice before bed, and, if all else fails, count the Flopsy Bunnies instead of sheep while you drop off.

Vital ingredients:
calcium and magnesium

Best juices:
banana, grapefruit

Best vegetables:
lettuce, carrot, celery

Tropical Hit

This interesting blend has a great flavor and would be an excellent breakfast juice. It provides enough of a punch to help cure a hangover, too! The enzyme bromelain in the pineapple will calm churning stomachs, the oranges will replace lost vitamin C, and the melon will help restore fluid levels.

Ingredients

2 oranges

One quarter of a yellow melon

Quarter of pineapple

1 kiwi fruit

Method

Peel the oranges and break into segments. Peel the kiwi fruit and remove the pineapple flesh from the skin. Remove the seeds from the melon and cut the flesh away from the skin. Juice each fruit and add the juice to a tall glass. Stir, and garnish with a slice of orange.

Brain Blaster

Scientists have determined that we use, on average, only 10 percent of the brain. This juice should help stimulate the remaining 90 percent, so prepare for an amazingly cerebral day!

Ingredients

1 orange
1 pear
1 grapefruit
1 apple

Method

Peel the orange and the grapefruit and break into segments to fit the feeder tube. Chop up the apple and pear so that they fit the feeder tube and juice, pits, skin and all. Pour into a glass and garnish with a slice of orange.

Orange Dawn

A simple juice with the energizing zing of orange matched by
the floral flavors of peach.

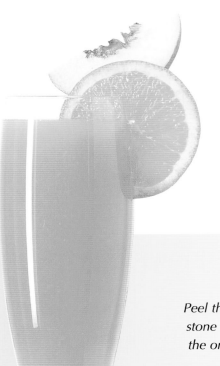

Ingredients
1 peach
2 oranges

Method

*Peel the oranges and break into segments. Remove the
stone from the peach and juice with the skin on. Juice
the orange, combine the juices in a glass, and garnish
with a slice of orange.*

Pink Blast

The deep pink color alone is enough to open your bleary eyes, and the flavor will send a shot of vitamin C and energizing electrolytes through your system.

Ingredients

An eighth of a watermelon

5 oz (150 g) strawberries

Method

Scrub the watermelon and juice it complete with skin and pits. Remove the stalks from the strawberries and add to the juicer. Combine the juices in a glass and garnish with a strawberry on a cocktail stick.

Blackberry and Pear

This is a healthy variation on one of my favorite pie fillings. It is a deep purple color and the flavor is redolent of warm September afternoons in the garden. An excellent juice for a fall morning.

Ingredients

2 pears

5 oz (150 g) blackberries

Method

Rinse the blackberries and chop the pears to fit the juicer, perhaps leaving a slice for garnish. Combine the juices in a tumbler and enjoy.

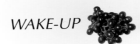

Ginger Grapes

This refreshing juice is a great way to start the day. It will clear your head and cleanse your system.

Ingredients

About 25 red grapes

2 inches(5 cm) fresh ginger, peeled

1 lemon, peeled

3.5 fl oz (100 ml) water to dilute – sparkling or still

Method

Rinse the grapes, peel and chop the lemon to fit the feeder tube, reserving a twist of peel for garnish, if you choose. Peel the ginger. Juice the ingredients and combine in a glass. Top up with sparkling water.

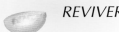

Mild Melon

An excellent restorative drink. Add a sprinkling of ground ginger if you are suffering from queasiness, or mix with sparkling water and crushed ice for a longer drink on a hot day.

Ingredients
Half a melon
2 oranges

Method

Peel the oranges and break into segments. Remove the melon from its skin and chop into chunks. Add to the juicer and combine the juices in a glass. Decorate with a chunk of melon and a slice of orange on a cocktail stick.

Pineapple, Melon, Banana Smoothie

Juice the pineapple, followed by the melon, and then pour the juice into a blender. Add the banana to produce a smoothie with all the flavors of the Caribbean.

Ingredients

Half a pineapple

Quarter of yellow melon

1 banana

Method

Remove the pineapple flesh from the tough skin and cut the melon flesh away from the rind; discard the seeds. Juice each fruit and add the juice to a blender. Chop the banana into chunks and add to the blender. Whiz until everything is smoothly combined, and then pour into a glass. Decorate with a small pineapple chunk.

Orange and Raspberry

The vibrant color of this juice will cheer you on a dull day, and the
vitamin C hit will boost energy levels.

Ingredients
2 oranges
5 oz (150 g) raspberries

Method

Peel the oranges and break into segments.
Rinse the raspberries. Juice each fruit and
combine the juices in a glass. Decorate with
a couple of raspberries on a cocktail stick.

Apple and Carrot

A creamy fruit and vegetable blend, with a hint of mint.

Ingredients

2 carrots

1 apple

1 sprig of mint

Method

Scrub the carrots, and remove the top and tail. Cut the apple into chunks. Juice the mint first and then add the other ingredients to the juicer, combining them all in a glass. Garnish with a sprig of mint.

Refuel

Refuel, revive, and recollect your thoughts by sipping this tangy drink.

Ingredients

*Slice of watermelon
(about 2 in or 5 cm
at widest point)*

2 oranges

*Quarter of
pineapple*

Method

*Peel the oranges and break into segments. Chop the
watermelon into chunks to fit the feeder tube – many
people like to juice the skin along with the flesh. (There
is certainly no need to remove the pits!) Remove the
pineapple flesh from the skin. Juice the ingredients one
by one and combine the juice in a tall glass.*

After Eight

After you have made this juice, you might like to blend it with some ice for a really long, cool drink, perfect to perk you up after a long day.

Ingredients

3 kiwi fruit

1 apple

*8 sprigs mint
(leaves and stems)*

Method

Juice the mint, reserving a small sprig. Peel the kiwi fruit and chop to fit the feeder tube. Juice. Chop the apple and juice. Combine the ingredients in a glass and decorate with the mint.

Liquid Lunch

Use this powerful juice if you have missed lunch. It is a hearty combination
that is an excellent meal-substitute. If you prefer a sweeter flavor,
add two oranges to the blend.

Ingredients
2 carrots
Half a cucumber
2 stalks celery
Half a beetroot

Method
*Scrub the carrots and celery, and top and tail them.
Scrub the beetroot thoroughly and slice the fibrous stalk
off the bottom. Juice the beetroot, followed by the
carrots and then the celery and finally the cucumber.
(With a bit of luck, the cucumber juice will flush the
violent beetroot and carrot colors through the juicer.)
Combine the juices in a glass and plant a stalk of
celery in it for garnish.*

Spiced Beetroot

An excellent juice to restore lost energy after a hard morning's work. The beetroot will help repair the body's iron levels and build up your strength for whatever the afternoon throws at you.

Ingredients

2 carrots

1 orange

Quarter of a beetroot

1 inch (2 cm) piece of fresh ginger

Method

Scrub the carrots and top and tail them. Scrub the beetroot thoroughly and slice the fibrous stalk off the bottom. Peel the orange and break into chunks. Juice the beetroot, followed by the carrots and then the ginger and orange. Combine the juices in a glass and garnish with an orange slice.

Barbados Breezer

A tangy, revitalizing juice, perfect to sip at the end of a long day. The mild melon calms frazzled nerves and the bromelain in the pineapple will soothe tense digestive tracts. Lie back, sip your juice and imagine a gentle Caribbean breeze wafting over a warm beach!

Ingredients

Half a pineapple
Half a melon
1 kiwi fruit

Method

Peel the kiwi fruit and chop it into chunks. Remove the pineapple flesh from the skin and do the same to the melon. Juice the ingredients one by one and combine the juice in a tall glass. Garnish with a slice of kiwi fruit.

Pink Pear

This has a finely balanced flavor; the grapefruit ensures that it is not too sweet, and if poured over crushed ice, it makes a great aperitif.

Ingredients

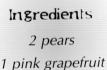

2 pears
1 pink grapefruit

Method

Remove the stalks from the pears and chop into chunks. Peel the grapefruit and break up to fit the feeder tube. Combine the juices in a glass, and decorate with a slice of pear and a grapefruit segment on a cocktail stick.

Orange Pear

Another excellent juice to help you unwind.

Ingredients

3 oranges

1 pear

Method

Peel the oranges and break into segments. Remove the woody stalk from the pear and chop into chunks. Juice the fruits and combine the juice in a glass. Garnish by floating slices of orange and pear on the top.

Red Mist

Juice the ingredients and then blend with some ice to produce an amazingly colorful slushy drink. Drink it to dispel the red mist of anger that may be hovering over you after an especially fraught day.

Ingredients

1 beetroot
2 apples
Half a lemon

Method

Scrub the beetroot thoroughly and slice the fibrous stalk off the bottom. Peel the lemon and chop the apples into chunks. Juice the beetroot, followed by the apples and then the lemon. Combine the juices in a glass and garnish with a slice of lemon.

Grapefruit and Blackcurrant

Juice the apple, blackcurrants and grapefruit, pour into a long glass
and sip slowly.

Ingredients

1 grapefruit

1 apple

*2.5 oz (75 g)
blackcurrants*

Method

*Peel the grapefruit and chop into chunks. Rinse the
blackcurrants and remove from the stalk. Chop up
the apple. Juice the blackcurrants, followed
by the grapefruit and then the apple. Combine the
juices in a glass and dangle a small stalk of
blackcurrants over the edge of the glass.*

Broccoli and Cucumber

Broccoli is not the juiciest of vegetables, but persevere and feed a cucumber into the juicer immediately after it to flush through the dark green goodness of the crucifer.

Ingredients

1 cucumber

4 stalks of broccoli

1 carrot

Method

Break up the broccoli florets so they will fit the feeder tube; scrub the carrot and slice off the ends. Juice the broccoli, followed by the carrot and finally the cucumber. Stir the juices together in a glass and garnish.

Popeye's Sundowner

After a hard day battling with Brutus, Popeye returned home to find that
Olive Oyl had prepared him a special cocktail to take his mind off
his troubles and reduce his aggression. . .

Ingredients
2 oranges
5–7 spinach leaves

Method
Peel the oranges and break into segments. Rinse
the spinach leaves thoroughly. Juice both
ingredients and mix the juices in a glass.
Garnish with a slice of orange.

Super Stress Reliever

This deep red juice is bursting with enzymatic goodness and will replenish the body's mineral levels. Garnish with the celery stalk and enjoy this cocktail of C and B vitamins.

Ingredients

1 broccoli floret
1 tomato
Half a red pepper
1 carrot
1 stalk of celery
Small handful of parsley
Celery stalk for garnish

Method

Break up the broccoli florets so they will fit the feeder tube; scrub the carrot and slice off the ends. Cut the tomato into quarters. Cut the pepper in half and discard the stalk. Rinse the celery and slice off the top and tail. Juice the broccoli, followed by the pepper, carrot, celery, parsley, and tomato. Stir the juices together and plant another stalk of celery in the glass for decoration.

Raspberry Nectar

This is a most seductive juice, and as the ingredients are rich in B vitamins, may well prove to be an admirable aphrodisiac.

Ingredients
6 oz (175 g) raspberries
2 peaches

Method
Rinse the raspberries and juice them. Cut the peach into quarters and remove the stone. Juice and add to the raspberry juice in a short glass. Using a cocktail stick make a small 'kebab' with two raspberries and a slice of peach to decorate.

Pineapple Berries

Iron-rich raspberries will soon restore your flagging energy levels.

Ingredients

Half a pineapple
5 oz (150 g) raspberries

Method

Rinse the raspberries and juice them.
Cut the pineapple flesh from the skin
and juice. Stir the fruit juices together
in a decorative glass – pour over
crushed ice for a really refreshing effect.

Mango Fix

Before juicing, inhale the glorious floral fragrance of the mango and then, once it has been pulverized along with the pineapple, enjoy the tangy taste of this energy-enhanced juice.

Ingredients
1 mango
Half a pineapple

Method

Cut the pineapple flesh from the skin and juice. Remove the stone from the mango by slicing it into quarters. It is perfectly safe to juice the skin, though you might prefer to wash it before doing so. Stir the juices together in a glass garnished with a slice of pineapple.

Carrot, Spinach, Avocado

Juice the spinach and carrot, then pour the juice into a blender with the avocado flesh. The ingredients combine to make a smoothie packed with energy. Add a dash of chilli sauce such as Tabasco if you wish to liven it up.

Ingredients

3 carrots

5–7 spinach leaves

Half an avocado

Method

Scrub the carrots and slice off the tops and tails. Rinse the spinach leaves and juice them, followed by the carrot. Cut the avocado in half and remove the stone. Add the carrot and spinach juices to a blender with the avocado and blend until smooth.

Spinach, Nutmeg and Carrot

The nutmeg somehow lends a Christmassy air to this refreshing juice. Don't wait till you're bowled over by the stress of the Yuletide season, however.

Ingredients
3 carrots
5–7 spinach leaves
Freshly grated nutmeg

Method
Scrub the carrots and slice off the tops and tails. Rinse the spinach leaves and juice them, followed by the carrot. Mix the juices in a glass and grate some fresh nutmeg over the top.

Broccoli and Apple

The sweetness of the apple is perfectly counterbalanced by the more savoury broccoli. This is a juice to restore and refresh you.

Ingredients

2 apples
4 florets broccoli

Method

Cut up the apples to fit the feeder tube and break up the broccoli florets. Juice the broccoli, followed by the apple and decorate with a couple of apple slices.

Watercress, Carrot and Cucumber

A slightly peppery concoction, which harnesses the iron-rich properties of watercress to boost energy levels.

Ingredients

2 carrots

Large handful watercress

Half a cucumber

Method

Scrub the carrots and slice off the tops and tails. Rinse the watercress and juice them, followed by the carrot and then the cucumber. Mix the juices in a glass and decorate with a few stems of watercress.

Mango, Banana and Orange

Juice the mango and the orange, then add to a blender with the chopped banana. Sip slowly while enjoying some wholemeal toast and retire to bed.

Ingredients

1 mango
1 banana
1 orange

Method

Remove the stone from the mango by slicing it into quarters. It is safe to juice the skin, though you should wash the fruit first. Peel the orange and break into quarters. Roughly chop the banana. Juice the mango and the orange and add the juices to a blender with the banana and blend until smooth.

Melon and Banana

Juice the melon and add the juice to a blender with the chopped banana.

Ingredients
Half a yellow melon
1 banana

Method
Cut the melon in half and remove the seeds. Remove the flesh from the skin and add to the juicer. Roughly chop the banana. Add the melon juice and the banana to a blender and blend until smooth.

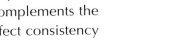

Grapefruit and Kiwi

This provides magnesium, essential to boost the enzyme processes necessary for hormonal equilibrium. The smooth kiwi fruit complements the tangy grapefruit juice, making a juice with the perfect consistency for drowsy sipping.

Ingredients

1 grapefruit
3 kiwi fruit

Method

Peel the grapefruit and break into segments. Remove the skin from the kiwi fruits and chop into chunks; save a slice for decoration. Juice the grapefruit and then the kiwis and stir the juices together in a glass. Decorate with a slice of kiwi fruit.

Snoozing Rabbit

Juice the ingredients, drink and dream of summer days and newly mown lawns!

Ingredients
3 carrots
Half a small lettuce

Method
Scrub the carrots and top and tail them.
Rinse the lettuce leaves and shake them dry.
Juice the ingredients and mix in a glass.

Celery, Lettuce and Cucumber

More rabbit food, fit for a tired bunny. This is a particularly cool drink, and might help when sleep eludes you on a humid summer's evening.

Ingredients

3 stalks of celery
Half a small lettuce
Half a cucumber

Method

Rinse the celery thoroughly and chop off the tops and tails. Rinse the lettuce and shake dry. Chop the cucumber to fit the feeder tube. Juice the ingredients and combine in a glass. Decorate with another celery stalk.

Celery, Carrot and Watercress

Celery and watercress also contain calcium and magnesium to calm the nervous system. Mix with carrot for a healthy alternative to bedtime cocoa!

Ingredients

2 carrots
2 stalks of celery
Handful of watercress

Method

Scrub the carrots and top and tail them. Rinse the celery thoroughly and chop off the tops and tails. Wash the watercress. Juice the ingredients and combine in a glass, using a sprig of watercress for garnish.

Cauliflower and Carrot

Cauliflower is rich in vitamin B3 (niacin), which helps maintain hormone levels to balance the neurotransmitters in the brain. Juice the cauliflower and carrots and decorate with the parsley sprig.

Ingredients

5 oz (150 g) cauliflower
2 carrots
Sprig of parsley

Method

Scrub the carrots and top and tail them. Break the cauliflower into florets and juice, followed by the carrots and a little parsley. Mix the ingredients in a glass. Finely chop another sprig of parsley and sprinkle over the top of the drink.

Celery Sleepover

The best possible blend of vegetables for a good night's sleep. This mild juice will soothe a frazzled system and calm an overwrought mind.

Ingredients
Half a small lettuce
2 carrots
2 sticks of celery

Method
Scrub the carrots and top and tail them. Wash the lettuce thoroughly and shake dry. Rinse the celery and remove the tops and tails. Juice the carrots, followed by the celery and then the lettuce. Garnish with a stick of celery if desired.

Top to Toe Health

For centuries herbalists and doctors harnessed the healing power of fruit, vegetables, and herbs – in the days before conventional medicine, it was all anybody could rely on. What is remarkable is that today many of these ancient cures have been found to have some basis in scientific fact. One of the earliest and greatest homeopathic treatises, Nicholas Culpepper's *Complete Herbal*, is still used by homeopaths and naturopaths today, and Culpepper, a 17th-century scholar and scientist, based much of his work on the studies of Galen, Hippocrates, and other classical authors. Culpepper attempted to show the influence of the planets on plants, illnesses and their cures, but some of his unscientific, not to say superstitious, theories have been reinforced in modern scientific research. Garlic, for example, has high levels of the element germanium, an antioxidant which promotes cellular uptake of oxygen, and is vital in the body's fight against cancer. It has also been shown to act as an anticoagulant, lowering blood pressure and cholesterol levels: these are facts which have been proved by controlled experiments and research in laboratories around the world. Meanwhile, 350 years ago, Culpepper wrote that garlic is "a remedy for all diseases and hurts".

"Then I considered that all medicines were compounded of Herbs, Roots, Flowers, Seeds, &c., and this first set me to work in studying. . ." Nicholas Culpepper

The vitamins and minerals in juices can be used to target different areas of the body, to improve the complexion, or tackle digestive problems, for example. If you suffer from a chronic disease or complaint, it is certainly worth supplementing your regular medical regime with a few juices – if your doctor concurs. Juice therapy has not been the subject of many controlled scientific studies, but as early as the 1950s, a report by the British Ministry of Health and Public Service Laboratory noted that

"Juices are valuable in relief of hypertension, cardiovascular and kidney diseases and obesity. Good results have been obtained . . . in the treatment of peptic ulceration, also in the treatment of chronic diarrhoea, colitis, and toxaemia of gastro and intestinal origin. . . The high buffering capacities of the juices reveal that they are very valuable in the treatment of hyperchlrohydria [excessive production of hydrochloric acid in the stomach]. Milk has often been used for this purpose, but spinach juice, juices of cabbage, kale and parsley were found to be superior to milk for this purpose."

Further studies have been carried out all over the world, notably in the U.S.A., where the British findings were reinforced by trials with raw cabbage juice at Stanford University Medical School.

Scientific research continues to reveal exactly what components in fruit and vegetables help to heal our bodies; in many cases science is reinforcing ancient folk cures. What is important is that by analyzing cell structure and dissecting the chemical make-up of fruit and vegetables, science has been able to pinpoint which chemical compounds fight disease and help our bodies to heal themselves.

The identification of phytonutrients, the organic components of plants that are thought to promote human health, has led to a greater understanding of how to harness fresh produce to protect physical well-being. Compounds such as carotenoids (the red, orange and yellow pigments that give color to some fruit and vegetables) appear to protect the body against some cancers, heart disease, and muscular degeneration in old age. They are antioxidants, which means they attack the rogue free radicals in cells known to cause aging and disease.

Enzymes in plants are proteins and are destroyed by cooking, so to fully absorb their goodness, plants are best eaten raw. Juicing concentrates the vitamins and minerals into an easily digestible form , allowing it all to be absorbed into the blood stream as quickly as ten minutes after consumption. Fresh juice is the best multivitamin supplement available and will help to replace the vital trace minerals and vitamins which are so often depleted by modern living and a diet of convenience foods.

Don't forget that you can drink any of the juices just for pure enjoyment – you really don't need an excuse! Or, as Culpepper said in a rather more grouchy tone. "Those that would live in health, may use it if they please; if they will not, I cannot help it".

Recipes are identified as follows:

Hair

Everyone suffers from bad hair days once in a while, but imbibing a combination of fruit and vegetable juices rich in B vitamins can restore that glossy, easy-to-manage look so beloved of the models in shampoo advertisements. Although we cannot beat our genetic predisposition to hair loss, we can try to delay the inevitable as long as possible. Sprouted alfalfa and cabbage both offer substantial protection. Use ingredients with high levels of iron, iodine and sulphur, such as tangerines, raspberries, and kale, to help restore your crowning glory.

Nails

When nails break or split it is annoying rather than tragic, but repetitive nail injury may result from mineral deficiencies. A lack of iron produces brittle nails, and white spots are a sign of zinc insufficiency.

Face and Skin

Our skin mirrors our health, and the way it looks has an important impact on our self-esteem. Aging cannot be prevented, however, and we should really rejoice in the wisdom and experience granted to us as we get older. However, vanity is never an entirely rational emotion, so if you would like to slow the visible effects of aging, while still rejoicing in the inner wisdom bestowed with the passing years, these juices are for you!

Wrinkles are caused when the skin begins to lose its elasticity as collagen levels decline. Antioxidants such as betacarotene, vitamins C and E, and the trace element selenium (present in leafy green vegetables) work to boost collagen and thus help the skin to retain its suppleness. Zinc, which is present in raspberries, watercress, broccoli, and tomatoes, is also important in the maintenance of healthy skin, as it promotes healing and repair.

Acne is usually the result of over-active sebaceous glands, combined with a digestive system blocked by an unhealthy diet. Detoxifying may provide an answer, by consuming juices that flush out the impurities from the body.

Eczema is an irritating skin condition which affects millions of people. Studies have shown that the worst effects can sometimes be alleviated by adapting one's diet. Many sufferers find that citrus fruits, spicy foods, and dairy produce worsen the condition.

Respiratory Problems

The boarding school I attended regularly served a tired concoction called "Winter Salad", which was essentially coleslaw with sultanas. It was very unedifying, but the nutritional intentions were good: raw cabbage and raw carrot contain many of the anti-oxidizing vitamins and minerals that fight colds and flu.

Everyone is plagued by the common cold, coughs, and other wheezes from time to time. Years of research have shown that we are more susceptible to colds and flu when our immune systems are run down, so by incorporating fresh juice into your diet, you are one step on the road to prevention.

Zinc has been shown to be helpful in combating colds, so if you feel the unwelcome symptoms coming upon you, concoct a juice rich in zinc, by using raspberries, lemon or blackcurrant, and broccoli, tomato, Brussels sprouts, and watercress. Vegetable recipes are particularly good, if only for the bracing effect that many of them provide.

Chronic respiratory problems, such as asthma, catarrh, hay fever, or other allergies can sometimes be alleviated by juices which help to build up reserves of vitamin C, betacarotene and the B vitamins, as well as zinc. Juices rich in magnesium may also prove helpful, to help control neuromuscular activity and relax the bronchial muscles; add a tablespoon or two of fresh lemon juice to keep asthma attacks at bay.

Digestion

Most people suffer from a minor digestive problem at some point, and as Culpepper noted rather unsympathetically, "Infirmities of the stomach usually proceed from surfeiting." He had a point, and today such "surfeiting" may also be identified as intolerance to certain foods.

Generally, the juices that work best to combat stomach problems are those rich in B vitamins, vitamin C, betacarotene and chlorine: carrots, cabbage, chicory, apples, citrus fruits, melon, pineapple, and raspberries. Mint and ginger make refreshing herbal additions.

Plain yogurt can also help soothe an upset stomach, so a fresh fruit smoothie is a delicious form of medicine. Yogurt containing the *lactobacillus bulgaricus* microbe ("live" yogurt) works to prevent incipient infections, regulate bowel function, and improve the absorption of B vitamins and calcium.

Heart and Circulation

Western diets that are high in sugar, fats, and refined food clog up arteries and cause heart attacks. So, if you do nothing else, use a few of the recipes in this book to replace calorie-rich snacks.

Women's Health and Pregnancy

Healthy bodies usually produce healthy babies, and medical professionals recommend that couples trying to conceive should live and eat as healthily as possible at least three months before conception. Women should ensure that they consume plenty of vegetables rich in folic acid, B complex vitamins and especially vitamin E, zinc, magnesium, and iron. Many doctors advise patients to cut down on tea, coffee, and alcohol because they inhibit the body's absorption of these vital minerals.

The early stage of pregnancy can be miserable if you suffer from morning sickness. The trick here is to train someone else to operate the juicer, so that you can approach the day slowly, beginning with a glass of fresh juice presented before you get out of bed. Try mild juices such as melon and ginger which may help alleviate the symptoms of nausea.

Energy levels often sag at the end of the day, especially in second or third pregnancies, so check the juices in chapter three for restorative drinks and try to find time to relax and enjoy them. Fresh juices can help maintain vitamin and mineral requirements, but it is important that pregnant women do not drink concentrated juices, so dilute the mixtures with still or sparkling water.

Premenstrual Syndrome

The symptoms of PMS range from irritability to stomach cramps to lethargy to dull skin blemishes, headaches, and fluid retention, occurring in the few days before a period. These changes probably stem from an imbalance between the hormones progesterone and oestrogen. Fruit juices rich in B vitamins may help to regulate hormonal imbalance, as will the minerals magnesium, iron, calcium, potassium, and zinc.

Urinary Problems

Water retention in women is often a hormonal problem, occurring at certain stages of the menstrual cycle. Juices high in sodium and potassium may help to alleviate the problem. Cranberries are famous for their diuretic properties, but strawberries, melons, celery and cucumber are also useful.

Cystitis is another unpleasant urinary problem which can be tackled very effectively with cranberry juice. Cranberries contain a potent mix of vitamins C and D, along with potassium and carotene, which helps to prevent E. coli bacteria attaching themselves to the walls of the urinary tract.

Prostate

Prostate problems afflict far more men than women. Troubling waterworks are neither pleasant nor dignified and the investigations into these problems even less so. Medical research into the anti-carcinogenic benefits of tomatoes, however, has shown that regular consumption can help prevent prostate cancer. Studies have shown that men who eat more than ten servings of tomatoes per week reduce their chance of contracting prostate cancer by 35 percent.

Aches and Pains

Persistent cramp or mystery pains may be a sign that trace minerals such as sodium and magnesium need boosting. The vitamins and minerals in fresh juice can help restore a battered body, even if you are suffering from fractures and bruises. Green leafy vegetables, and more especially, milk or yogurt are vital as they are packed with calcium which will help bones to heal more quickly; grapefruit are especially recommended for those recovering from operations.

Osteoporosis causes bones to become brittle and is a debilitating condition which affects many older people, especially women, as their bone mass deteriorates with age. It is a natural part of aging, but the worst effects can be minimized by eating a calcium-rich diet, preferably from your 30s onwards.

Back pain afflicts huge numbers of the population every year. Before you reach for the tablets, try a couple of juices which have the required anti-inflammatory and mildly analgesic effect necessary for pain relief.

Osteoarthritis and rheumatoid arthritis are more pernicious conditions which can also be partially alleviated by juice therapy. Pineapple, which contains the anti-inflammatory enzyme bromelain, is a good addition to the diet, as are grapes, apples, leafy green vegetables, carrots, leeks, beetroot, and ginger.

Raspberry Sunrise

Freeze some of the raspberries you pick in the summer and enjoy their restorative powers all year round. Tangerines are especially rich in vitamin B1 (thiamine), which helps maintain the health of hair follicles.

Ingredients

7 oz (200 g) raspberries

3 tangerines

Method

Peel the tangerines and break into segments. Rinse the raspberries. Juice each fruit and combine the juices in a glass.

Cherry and Orange Blossom

Luscious cherries, full of vitamin B2 (riboflavin) and betacarotene, are ideal for stimulating healthy hair. Mix with orange juice to make a long, refreshing drink.

Ingredients

4 oranges

Large handful cherries (about 12)

Method

Peel the oranges and break into quarters. Rinse the cherries and remove the stones (fiddly, but worthwhile) by cutting each one in half. Juice the cherries, followed by the oranges and combine in a glass. Decorate with a couple of cherries.

Kiwi Grapes

Grapes are full of vitamin E which will help restore the mineral balance to your scalp and hair follicles, and guard against dandruff.

Ingredients

5 oz (150 g) grapes
3 kiwi fruit

Method

Rinse the grapes and remove from the stalks. Peel the kiwi fruit and chop to fit the feeder tube. Reserve one slice for decoration. Juice the kiwis, then the grapes, and combine the juices in a glass. Decorate with a slice of kiwi fruit.

Watercress and Carrot Tickler

Watercress adds a slightly peppery flavor to the carrot juice; more importantly it is full of vitamins, and is especially well-endowed with sulfur and iron. The parsley is not just a decorative element – it is another powerful green vegetable which will cleanse your system.

Ingredients

4 carrots
Handful of watercress
2 sprigs of parsley

Method

Scrub the carrots and remove the tops and tails. Rinse the watercress and parsley, and juice. Juice the carrots and combine with the watercress and parsley in a glass. Decorate with a sprig of parsley.

Cabbage Cure

Cabbage is iron-rich and full of trace minerals which will help make
your hair glossy. The betacarotene in the carrots will improve
the overall condition of the scalp.

Ingredients
*4 oz (125 g)
Savoy cabbage
3 carrots*

Method
*Scrub the carrots and remove the
tops and tails. Rinse the cabbage,
chop roughly, and juice. Juice
the carrots and combine the
juices in a glass.*

Mange Tout Mender

Mange tout are legumes, which are an excellent source of zinc and other trace elements. The juice is bright green, so admire it briefly before diluting it with the carrot juice.

Ingredients

4 oz (125 g) mange tout

2 carrots

Method

Rinse the mange tout and top and tail them.
Top and tail the carrots, then scrub them. Juice
the produce and combine the juices in a glass.

Kiwik Fix

Raspberries are rich in zinc and kiwi fruit are an excellent source of vitamin B2, riboflavin, which is vital for strong nail growth.

Ingredients

2 kiwi fruit
4 oz (125 g) raspberries

Method

Rinse the raspberries and peel the kiwis, reserving a slice for decoration. Juice the raspberries, then the kiwis and swirl the juices together over some crushed ice for a decorative drink. Or simply mix the juices in a glass and float a thin slice of kiwi fruit on top.

Grape, Apple and Blackcurrant

Grapes and blackcurrants are full of vitamins E and C respectively,
the antioxidants that fight most efficiently the damaging effects of free radicals,
the agents of ageing.

Ingredients

5 oz (150 g) grapes

*5 oz (150 g)
blackcurrants*

1 apple

Method

*Rinse the blackcurrants and grapes and
remove the blackcurrants from their stems.
Remove stem from apple and cut into
chunks. Juice each ingredient and combine
the juices in a glass.*

Orange and Blackcurrant

A vitamin C-packed juice, with a fabulous mix of color. Try swirling it over crushed ice for a decorative effect.

Ingredients

2 oranges

*5 oz (150 g)
blackcurrants*

Method

*Peel the oranges and break into
quarters to fit the feed tube. Rinse the
blackcurrants and remove from their
stems. Juice each ingredient and
combine the juices in a glass*

Berry Blast

This is like liquid summer pudding. A delicious reviving summer drink.

Ingredients

5 oz (150 g)
blackcurrant

5 oz (150 g)
strawberries

Method

Rinse the blackcurrants and remove from their stems.
Rinse and hull the strawberries. Juice each ingredient
and combine the juices in a glass.

Parsley the Lion

Carrots have more betacarotene than anything else and are perfect antioxidants. Mixed with parsley and broccoli, they combine to make a juice rich in vitamins C and E which will nourish your collagen. Zinc in the broccoli will reinforce the skin's natural defenses.

Ingredients
3 carrots
4 broccoli florets
Handful of parsley

Method

Roughly chop the carrots and break the broccoli into chunks. Reserve a sprig of parsley for decoration. Juice each ingredient and combine the juices in a glass. Garnish with a sprig of parsley.

Avocado, Tomato, Coriander

This is guacamole in a glass, and no less delicious. Excellent for the skin, avocados are packed with goodness.

Ingredients

Half an avocado (stone removed)

4 tomatoes

2 sprigs of coriander

Method

Remove the stone from the avocado and scoop out the flesh. Combine the ingredients in a blender (avocados do not juice well) and garnish with a sprig of coriander.

Tomato and Watercress

Tomato juice laced with watercress and parsley makes a refreshing, slightly peppery concoction, which will protect the skin in several ways, first by detoxifying and second by re-establishing hormonal equilibrium via the zinc which is present in both tomatoes and watercress.

Ingredients

4 tomatoes

Large handful of watercress

Two stalks of parsley

Method

Chop the tomatoes into quarters. Juice the watercress and parsley, followed by the tomatoes. Mix the juices in a glass.

Raspberry Reviver

Raspberries are rich in zinc which helps to control the activity of the sebaceous glands. The melon will help detoxify your system.

Ingredients

5 oz (150 g) raspberries

Quarter melon

1 apple

Method

Scoop out the pips from the melon and remove the skin. Rinse the raspberries and quarter the apple. Juice the raspberries, then the apple and finally the melon. Combine the juices in a tall glass.

Cranberry and Raspberry

Cranberries are well-known for their diuretic properties and this ruby-red juice will help re-establish the equilibrium necessary for healthy skin.

Ingredients

5 oz (150 g) cranberries
5 oz (150 g) raspberries

Method

Rinse the berries and add to the juicer
Mix the juices together in a glass

Melon Surprise

The surprise is the simplicity of this juice. Rich in betacarotene and bio-flavonoids, melon is a mild juice which should help relieve the itchiness associate with eczema.

Ingredients

Half a yellow melon

Method

Cut the rind away from the flesh. Add flesh (and seeds) to the juicer and enjoy.

The Soothing Green One

This juice is rich in zinc and other trace minerals, which helps the skin to recover from an eczema attack. Zinc is particularly important as it helps wounds to heal, and the iron present in the watercress promotes good skin tone.

Ingredients

¾ cucumber

Half an avocado
(stone removed)

Handful of watercress

Sprig of parsley

Method

Remove the stone from the avocado and scoop the flesh into the blender. Either juice the cucumber and watercress and add the juices to a blender with the avocado, or put all the ingredients in the blender and whiz to a smooth consistency.

Cold Salad

Try this when you feel the symptoms of an unwelcome cold catching up with you. Zinc-rich tomatoes will strengthen the immune system and the betacarotene and vitamin C in the lettuce and carrots will beat off germs.

Ingredients

2 carrots

Half a lettuce (or one little gem lettuce)

2 tomatoes

Method

Top and tail the carrots, rinse the lettuce leaves and halve the tomatoes. Juice the tomatoes, carrots and lettuce and combine the juices in a tall glass.

The Three Cs

Packed with energizing chlorophyl, the plant compound that closely resembles hemoglobin, this juice will speed recovery by restoring iron levels in the blood.

Ingredients

Quarter of a Savoy cabbage

Half a cucumber

2 carrots

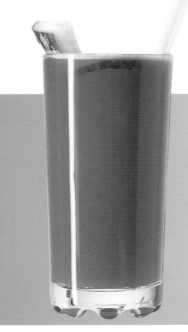

Method

Top and tail the carrots, rinse and roughly chop the cabbage leaves and chop the cucumber into chunks. Reserve a slice of cucumber for decoration. Add the ingredients to the juicer and combine the juices in a tall glass.

Allium Appetizer

This is based on a recipe in *The Juicing Bible* by Pat Crocker and Susan Eagles and is only for those whose senses are so dulled by a cold that their taste buds are all but dead! It is very strong, but is packed with concentrated antioxidants and antibacterial goodies. If it really is too powerful, try adding more apple juice.

Ingredients

2 apples
2 stalks celery
Half an onion
1 clove garlic
1 stalk broccoli

Method

Remove the rooty part of the celery, roughly chop the onion, apple and broccoli. Add the ingredients to the juicer and combine the juices in a tall glass.

Garlic Gargle

Harness the antioxidant and antiviral properties of garlic to ward off cold germs (and unwanted attention). Eating raw garlic undoubtedly strengthens the immune system, and the betacarotene of the carrots helps to tone the mucus membranes and eases breathing.

Ingredients

2 cloves garlic

4 carrots

3 sprigs parsley

Method

Top and tail the carrots, and peel the papery skin off the garlic. Juice two sprigs of parsley, followed by the remaining ingredients and combine the juices in a tall glass. Decorate with a sprig of parsley.

Blackcurrant, Lemon and Apple

This is a juiced version of all those powders available on the shelves at the pharmacy. It will taste much better, will revive a palate jaded by a stuffed nose, and generally make you feel brighter. More importantly, the high concentration of vitamin C will help combat persistent bugs.

Ingredients

3 apples

1 lemon

2.5 oz (75 g) blackcurrants

Method

Remove the skin from the lemon (but leave as much pith as possible). Rinse the blackcurrants and roughly chop the apples to fit the feeder tube. Add the ingredients to the juicer and combine the juices in a glass, using a sprig of blackcurrants or a slice of lemon for decoration.

Apricot Antioxidant

Packed with betacarotene, the antioxidants in this juice will help tackle the most persistent cold bugs. It is such a great color that it will cheer you up if you are contemplating a cold, damp, winter's day, too.

Ingredients

4 apricots

1 mango

1 orange

Method

Remove the stones from the apricots and the mango. Dig out the mango pulp with a spoon and add to the juicer, followed by the apricots. Remove the skin from the orange and break into segments prior to juicing. Combine the juices in a tall glass.

Apricot and Tangerine Trio

Another delicious combination of betacarotene and antioxidants to demolish your wintry ills.

Ingredients

4 apricots

1 pear

2 tangerines

Method

Remove the stones from the apricots, cut the woody stem off the pear and take the skin off the tangerines. Juice the apricots, tangerines, and the pear and mix the juices in a glass.

Citrus and Berry Blast

A really delicious, reviving juice. Don't wait until you have a cold to try it!

Ingredients
1 lemon

2 oranges

4 oz (125 g) raspberries

Method
Remove the skin from the oranges and lemon and break into segments. Rinse the raspberries and juice them, followed by the oranges. and the lemon.

Carrot and Ginger

Carrot juice is naturally sweet, but here it is enlivened by the flavor of fresh ginger. Ginger has been used for centuries as a cure for nausea, so, if you feel a little queasy, try this.

Ingredients

4 carrots

¾-in (2 cm) piece of ginger

Method

Scrub the carrots (or peel them if you prefer) and chop to fit the juicer. Peel the ginger. Juice the ingredients and mix in a tall glass. Sip slowly.

Gingered Melon

This mild blend of melon and ginger is perfect for nausea and may be helpful to women suffering from morning sickness. Add sparkling water if you prefer a longer, more diluted drink.

Ingredients

Half a cantaloupe or Charantais melon

³/₄ in (2 cm) piece of ginger

Method

Scoop the seeds from the melon and remove the skin. Peel the ginger. Juice the ingredients and mix in a tall glass. Sip slowly

Tropical Cabbage

Cabbage is excellent for stomach disorders, but even its most ardent advocates admit that the flavor leaves something to be desired. Fresh cabbage juice is often recommended for sufferers of stomach ulcers, but it is probably preferable to mix it with something more palatable.

Ingredients

*Quarter of a
Savoy cabbage*

Half a pineapple

Method

Rinse the cabbage leaves and remove the skin and core from the pineapple. Juice the cabbage, then the pineapple, and whisk the juices together in a glass.

Apple Spritzer

Apples are an excellent cure for a stomach suffering from an excess of fatty or spicy foods. Use this juice if you are suffering from diarrhea, perhaps diluted with more water.

Ingredients

2 apples

2 fl oz(50 ml)
sparkling water
(or top up to taste)

Method

Chop the apples to fit the juicer and juice.
Mix with sparkling water to taste.

Pineapple Smoothie

The bromelain in pineapple helps to balance the acidity and alkalinity levels in the stomach. Yogurt, especially live yogurt, will help restore the bacterial levels in the gut after a bout of diarrhea or vomiting.

Ingredients

Half a pineapple

5 fl oz (150 g) plain yogurt

Water to dilute (optional)

Method

Remove the rind from the pineapple and roughly chop the flesh so it fits the juicer. Add the juice and the yogurt to a blender and whiz until smooth. If the idea of cleaning two sets of utensils appals you, simply add the chopped pineapple to the blender with the yogurt. The juice will simply be thicker. Stir in sparkling water if desired.

Grapefruit Smoothie

This is especially refreshing and will revive a constitution made groggy by digestive upheavals.

Ingredients

2 grapefruit

5 fl oz (150 g) plain yogurt

Water to dilute (optional)

Method

Peel the grapefruit and break in chunks to fit the juicer. Add the juice and the yogurt to a blender and whiz until smooth. Again, you could just add all the ingredients to the blender to produce a slightly thicker, but still delicious blend.

Spinach Shifter

Constipation is another miserable problem, resulting from a lack of fiber and a diet high in over-processed foods. All fresh juices will relax the bowels, but leafy green vegetables which are mineral-rich are especially useful.

Ingredients

3 tomatoes

3 large spinach leaves

1 carrot

Method

Rinse the spinach and scrub the carrot thoroughly. Juice the spinach, followed by the carrot and the tomato, and combine the juices in a glass.

Blood Orange Thinner

Help prevent clogged arteries with this deliciously tangy citrus blend.

Ingredients
2 oranges
1 grapefruit

Method

Peel the skin from the oranges and grapefruit (but leave as much pith as possible). Break into segments and add the ingredients to the juicer. Combine the juices in a glass.

Potassium Power Punch

Both blackcurrants and spinach are full of potassium which
helps control blood pressure.

Ingredients

*5 oz (150 g)
blackcurrant*

6 leaves spinach

2 oranges

Method

*Rinse the blackcurrants and remove the stalks. Reserve
a stalk for decoration. Peel the oranges and break into
segments. Juice the blackcurrants, spinach and oranges
and combine the juices in a glass. Decorate with a
blackcurrant stalk.*

Green Apple Cocktail

Vitamin E deficiency may lead to a decline in reproductive powers, so plenty of watercress will boost the body's levels.

Ingredients
Large bunch watercress
3 apples

Method

Rinse the watercress and chop the apples. Juice the watercress and then the apples, mixing the juices together in a glass.

Orange Cress

This peppery orange concoction is not only full of fertility enhancing nutrients, but will also boost energy levels.

Ingredients

4 oranges

Large bunch of watercress

Method

Rinse the watercress and peel the oranges, before breaking them into segments. Juice the watercress followed by the oranges and mix the juices in a glass.

Apricot Abundance

This juice is full of betacarotenes, vitamin E and the minerals necessary to impose optimum health on your reproductive system.

Ingredients

4 apricots

Half a mango

2 oranges

Method

Cut the apricots in half and remove the stones. Juice them first. Remove the stone from the mango and scoop the flesh into the juicer. Peel the oranges and break into segments. Juice the mango, followed by the orange and combine them in a glass

Fertile Pear

Melons have always been symbolically associated with fertility and their image is reinforced by the goodness inherent within them. Pears are rich in folic acid and melons have a gentle cleansing effect on the body, so this is a good juice if you are preparing for conception.

Ingredients

1 pear

Half a cantaloupe melon

Method

Remove the woody stem from the pear and chop into quarters. Scoop the seeds from the melon and cut off the rind. Juice the pear, followed by the melon and combine the juices in a glass.

Citrus Crucifer

This compelling combination is full of folic acid, the vitamin so vital in the prevention of birth defects in developing fetuses.

Ingredients
4 oranges
2.5 oz (75 g) broccoli

Method

Rinse the broccoli and juice it. Peel the oranges and break into segments. Juice them and mix the orange juice with the broccoli juice in a tall glass.

Folic Frolic

Delicious, summery, and extremely good for you – but being pregnant is optional!

Ingredients

Half a melon (Galia or cantaloupe)

4 oz (100 g) strawberries

Method

Remove the pips and skin from the melon. Rinse and hull the strawberries and add them to the juicer. Juice the melon and mix the juices in a glass.

Tangerine Dream

Tangerines and strawberries are not exactly a seasonally harmonious combination, but if you can get hold of strawberries in the winter, this is a delicious drink packed with folic acid and other trace minerals.

Ingredients
4 tangerines

7 oz (200 g) strawberries

Method

Peel the tangerines and juice. Rinse and hull the strawberries and juice them, mixing the juice with the pale-orange tangerine juice in a tall glass.

Lemon and Ginger Breezer

This is a refreshing combination which might help banish morning sickness – or at least give you the energy to get out of bed.

Ingredients

2 pears
Juice of half a lemon
¾ in (2 cm) ginger

Method

Peel the ginger, remove the woody stem from the pear and chop roughly. Peel the lemon. Juice the ginger, pear, and lemon, and mix the juices in a glass.

Carrot and Apple

A simple delicious juice which provides energy and an excellent multivitamin boost.

Ingredients
2 apples
1 large carrot

Method

Scrub the carrots and top and tail them. Chop the apples. Juice the carrots and then the apples and mix the juices in a glass.

Carrots and Broccoli

An excellent source of magnesium and betacarotene, this drink will invigorate a weary body.

Ingredients

3 carrots

3.5 oz (100 g) broccoli

Method

Rinse the broccoli and juice it. Scrub the carrots and top and tail them. Add to the juicer and combine the juices in a glass.

Peppery Apples

An amazingly flavorsome juice, with the slightly peppery taste of the watercress enhancing the sweetness of the apples. Green peppers are full of vitamin B6 (pyridoxine) which helps alleviate the problems of water retention.

Ingredients

1 green pepper

3 apples

Small handful of watercress

Method

Remove the top and seeds from the pepper. Rinse the watercress and roughly chop the apples. Reserve a sprig of watercress for decoration. Juice the pepper, followed by the watercress and then the apple. Combine the juices in a glass and trail a stem of watercress around the glass.

Kiwi Pear

This green juice is packed with trace minerals and should help to stabilize the hormonal roller coaster.

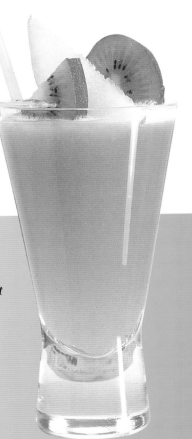

Ingredients

2 kiwi fruit
2 pears

Method

Peel the kiwis and juice. Chop the stalk off the pears, cut into chunks and juice. Stir the juices together in a tall glass and decorate with a slice of kiwi fruit.

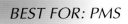

Kiwi and Banana Smoothie

Rich in vitamin B6 which promotes healthy skin, this juice also contains a good source of magnesium.

Ingredients
5 kiwis
1 ripe banana

Method

Peel the kiwis and juice. Chop the banana and either mash it with the kiwi juice, or add the kiwi juice and banana to a blender and whiz until smooth.

Cranberry Cure

A glorious pink juice which is a joy to behold and even better to drink.

Ingredients

7 oz (200 g) cranberries

large chunk of
watermelon
about 3 in (7 cm)
at widest part

Method

Rinse the cranberries and juice. Remove
the rind from the watermelon (optional) and
juice the seeds and flesh. Combine the
juices in a glass.

Watermelon Waterfall

Watermelon rind contains chlorophyl, vitamin A, protein, potassium, zinc, iodine, nucleic acids, and enzymes which aid digestion. Ninety-five percent of the nutritional content in watermelon is in the rind. The seeds may be a little noisy but are harmless to the juicer.

Ingredients

5 oz (150 g) red grapes

Watermelon wedge about 3 in (7 cm) at widest part

Method

Rinse the grapes and reserve a couple for decoration. Chop the watermelon to fit the juicer (remove the rind if you prefer). Juice the grapes and then the watermelon. Combine the juices in a glass and garnish with a couple of grapes.

Red Spuds

Potatoes do not immediately spring to mind when one thinks of juicing, but the pale juice is rich in minerals and folic acid.

Ingredients

1 potato (about 2 oz or 50 g)

5 tomatoes

sprig of parsley

Method

Scrub the potato thoroughly (peel if it's very dirty) and add to the juicer. Juice the tomatoes and mix with the potato juice. Finely chop the parsley and sprinkle over the top of the juice.

Super Stalks

Harness the potassium-rich celery and the flavonoid-filled tomatoes in this juice to protect against cancer-causing free-radical damage.

Ingredients
3 stalks celery
Half a cucumber
3 tomatoes

Method
Trim the leafy tops from two of the celery stalks. Roughly chop the cucumber and the tomatoes. Juice the celery, followed by the tomatoes, and finally the celery. Combine the juices in a glass and stir vigorously with the remaining celery stalk.

Green Melon

Melons are a particularly watery fruit, and so are a gentle diuretic. The minerals in this juice (magnesium and potassium) work to balance the hormonal system, and the cruciferous broccoli contains anti-cancer nutrients.

Ingredients

1 apple
Half a melon
3.5 oz (100 g) broccoli

Method

Chop the apple, scoop out the melon seeds, and remove the skin. Rinse the broccoli. Juice each item in turn and mix the juices in a glass.

Limber Up

Containing potassium and vitamins A and C, this juice may help relieve muscle ache and tension.

Ingredients

Half a cantaloupe melon

Half a lime

4 oz (125 g) grapes

Method

Scoop out the seeds and remove the melon from the skin. Rinse the grapes and add to the juice. Juice the lime, followed by the melon and mix the juices together in a glass.

Four Cs

This is rich in vitamins A and C, as well as sulfur. With calcium and iron, it is excellent for creaking bones.

Ingredients

2 carrots

3 leaves of Savoy cabbage

1 stick celery

Small handful of coriander

Method

Top and tail the carrots and roughly chop the cabbage. Add the cabbage to the juicer, followed by the coriander, celery, and finally the carrots.

Gingered Leek

Leeks are recommended for their cleansing, anti-inflammatory properties, and ginger stimulates the circulation, so the combination of the two may help ease joint pain.

Ingredients

1 small leek

3 apples

*¾ in (2 cm)
peeled ginger*

Method

*Top and tail the leek. Peel the outer ski
from the ginger and chop in hal
Chop the apples to fit the feeder tube
Juice the leeks, followed by th
ginger, then the apple*

Creak Juice

Another pain-busting combination to ease creaking joints.

Ingredients

2 leeks

2 carrots

Sprig of parsley
(reserve a little for
decoration)

Method

Top and tail the leeks and the carrots. Add to the
juicer, followed by the parsley. Combine the juices
in a glass, and garnish with a sprig of parsley.

Leeky Apple

Another juice designed to make you forget those lingering aches and pains.

Ingredients

1 leek

2 apples

2 stalks of celery,
with the leaves left on

Method

Top and tail the leek. Chop th
apples to fit the feeder tube. Juice th
leeks, followed by one stalk of celery
then the apple. Pour the juice into
glass and stir and garnish with th
remaining celery stalk

Bone Mender

Cabbages and onions are rich in calcium, so this juice is perfect if you are suffering from a broken bone. Calcium strengthens bones and will help fractures to heal more quickly.

Ingredients

2 apples

6 leaves Savoy cabbage

Half an onion

Freshly grated nutmeg

Method

Chop the apples, rinse the cabbage leaves, peel the onion and chop in half. Juice the onion, followed by the spinach and then the apple. Combine the juices in a glass and grate a little nutmeg over the top.

Spinach Strengthener

Spinach has a high calcium content. It also contains iron, so this recipe would be useful to soothe bruising.

Ingredients
3 leaves spinach

4 tomatoes

2 stalks celery

Method

Rinse the spinach leaves and chop the tomatoes
Juice the spinach, one stick of celery and th
tomatoes. Combine the juices in a glass an
garnish with the remaining stick of celer

Muscle Buster

This not recommended for those suffering from osteoarthritis, as some health therapists believe citrus juices contribute to joint inflammation. This juice and those on the following pages may soothe aching muscles.

Ingredients

Half a lemon
1 orange
1 pear
1 apple

Method

eserve half the lemon for decorative slices. Peel the
maining half along with the orange. Chop the apple
nd pear to fit the juicer. Juice the fruits and combine
he juices in a glass. Decorate with slices of lemon,
range and apple.

Cramp Beater

If you suffer from cramp, the ginger in this recipe may help improve your circulation, as will the sodium present in the kiwi fruit.

Ingredients

2 kiwi fruit

¾ in (2 cm) ginger, peeled and chopped roughly

2 apples

Method

Chop the apples and juice with the ginger. Top and tail the kiwis and remove the skin; reserve a slice for decoration. Juice the ginger and then the fruit and stir the juices together in a tall glass. Decorate with the slice of kiwi fruit.

Neat Pineapple

Harness the bromelain from the pineapple to soothe aching muscles and guard against bruising. This a terrific refreshing drink, a perfect reward after a long exercise session.

Ingredients

1 pineapple

Method

Remove the skin and core from the pineapple. Chop into chunks and juice.

Detox

There comes a time in everyone's life when they feel the need to shed a few pounds or do something to shake off a feeling of sluggishness and malaise. January is a popular time for resolutions of this nature, but often days of relentlessly gray and chilly weather do nothing to improve one's resolve. Winter for many is a time for hot drinks, chocolate cookies, and thick sweaters, not salad-based diets and inadequate lycra clothing. Juicing, however, is a perfect way to add color to those cold winter days and tropical fruits not only pep you up, but they also hint of the summer to come.

Detoxification in this context is the process of eliminating waste and built-up stores of toxins from your body. Harmful substances or "toxins" appear as the chemicals found in processed foods, such as additives, preservatives, and colors, as well as stimulants, such as alcohol, caffeine, nicotine, and artificial sweeteners. They are also present in the

Parsley tea. See page 179

environment, as pollution. A good detox cuts these toxins out completely. If you feel that you have not treated your body as the sacred temple it should be, it might be time to consider a day or so of detoxification, cutting out processed foods, sugars, caffeine, alcohol, and all those gastronomic props that shore up your life. A seasonal purge need not be a puritanical, miserable few days as you contemplate your empty stomach and cold, bare fridge. It can, given a little organization, be a time of pampering and contemplation, a period of getting in touch with your body and revitalizing it. Furthermore, it will improve many aspects of physical and mental well-being, such as vitality, immunity, fertility, sleep quality, and concentration. You will have extra energy and the appearance of skin and hair may be improved too.

So what are you waiting for?

Preparation

Try to set aside a day when you can concentrate on yourself, without having o worry about anyone else. Even a day of detoxification takes a bit of willpower, and it is best if you can ignore the needs of others and attend to your own activities. Eat as healthily as possible the day before, storing up reserves of simple foods such as vegetables, brown rice or pasta, bread, and pulses. Avoid processed foods, dairy products, and try to cut out caffeine, smoking, and alcohol.

A juice fast makes the whole process of digestion easier for your body; for 24 hours it only has to deal with healthy juices, so will only eliminate built-up waste from the body. You will probably need between four and six glasses of juice throughout the day, supplemented by water. You may develop a headache – a sign that your body is suffering withdrawal symptoms from caffeine, but it will probably pass as long as you keep yourself hydrated. However, with a bit of luck, you can do what you want, and it is the perfect time to pamper the body – take a long bath, book a massage or a reflexology treatment, or simply enjoy a long walk in the country. Do not plan to indulge in intensive exercise, because a 24-hour juice fast simply does not supply enough energy for violent athleticism. Instead, consider relaxation techniques, yoga, or meditation.

It is crucial that you drink plenty of water. A great many people are mildly dehydrated all the time, and this in turn leads to fatigue. Some doctors recommend drinking eight 8 fl oz (225 ml) glasses of water a day and this is especially true when you are detoxing as it helps to flush out your digestive system.

You will probably feel extra healthy and very relaxed at the end of your fast, but don't be tempted to extend it. You need a proper combination of foods to maintain good health, so return to a well-balanced diet, omitting processed, sugary or fatty items as far as possible. (See the appendix: A healthy diet on page 254.) A healthy person can probably incorporate a weekly juice fast into his or her diet. It will reduce stress, remove toxins, and leave you feeling reinvigorated.

Combative cleansers

Fruit juices are more efficient short-term cleansers than vegetable juices. Vegetable juices are more restorative, whereas acids in fruit work to cleanse the digestive system. Citrus fruits are the best, as citric acid is stronger than the tartaric or malic or acid present in other fruit. Vegetable juices are included in this chapter for those who feel that they need a gentle

Warning

Children, the elderly, pregnant women, or anyone with an existing medical condition should not consider a juice fast. If you are in any doubt about whether it is suitable for you, consult your doctor. Never fast for more than 24 hours at a time.

introduction to detoxifying their bodies. I have roughly divided the recipes into breakfast, lunch and dinner, but these are merely suggestions. Juice whatever you want when you want it! You may prefer to dilute the juices with 3.5 fl oz (100 ml) water – this will make the drink last longer and will lessen the effects of the natural sugars in the fruit juices, which may make you feel a little dizzy when they hit an empty stomach. Remember to sip the juices slowly; savor the taste and kid your stomach into thinking its receiving a full meal.

Parsley, peppermint, rosemary, ginger, oregano, garlic, chives, cucumber, leeks, and apples are among the best items to detoxify your body. Fresh wheatgrass is also useful as it is full of antioxidants and immune-boosting nutrients.

Juices are identified according to the best time to drink them.

Breakfast

Smoothies made with yogurt are excellent for breakfast as they provide extra energy to help you get through the day. These recipes are simple, yet effective – as well as being delicious. Try to use live yogurt because it contains *lactobacillus*, which helps to maintain a healthy balance of bacteria in the gut. Don't forget to have a couple of glasses of water during the morning, particularly if you succumb to a headache.

Lunch

Have lunch when you feel ready. You may well be feeling a little hungry, but take your time over sipping your juice, and you will soon feel revived. Take time after lunch to have a rest – fall asleep in front of the fire, watch a good film or read a gripping novel.

Dinner

By the evening you will probably feel wonderful, buoyed up by the satisfaction of a job well done. However, hunger pangs may also set in, but do not be tempted to reach for the cookie jar – you've spent a day purifying your body, so don't give in now. Enjoy a long juice at around 7pm and end the day with a herbal tea just before bed to ensure a good night's sleep.

Herbal Teas

Herbal teas are probably as old as Adam, and they are a useful addition to a detox regime. People all over the world have harnessed the aromatic and healing properties of herbs and spices for centuries to make warm, comforting drinks. Many can be combined with fruit juices to make restorative hot drinks, and some are even nicer if they are combined with the aromatic peel of citrus fruits. Fresh herbal teas are extremely easy to make and are far more refreshing than the rather dried-out herbal tea bags available in the supermarket.

Apple Smoothie

A mild, faintly tangy juice that will ease you into the morning. The addition of yogurt makes it a substantial drink that will provide energy for the day ahead.

Ingredients
1 apple

2 oranges

2.5 fl oz (75 ml) yogurt

about 10 mint leaves
(small sprig)

Method

Chop the apple and add to the juicer. Peel the oranges and juice. Combine the orange and apple juice in a glass. Add the juices and the yogurt to a blender and whiz until smooth. Finely chop the mint leaves and sprinkle over the top of the drink. If you prefer a longer drink, dilute with water.

Grapefruit Tonic

Grapefruits always make a refreshing start to the day. Here it is made milder by the apple juice.

Ingredients
1 apple
1 grapefruit

Method

Roughly chop the apple. Peel the grapefruit and break into segments. Juice the fruit and combine the juice in a glass. Mix with 5 fl oz (150 ml) of yogur if you prefer a more substantial drink

Pastel Citrus Cocktail

A bracing wake-up call that will fire you with enthusiasm and will-power!

Ingredients

1 pink grapefruit
2 oranges
Half a lemon

Method

Peel all the fruit and break into segments. Remember to retain as much pith as possible. Juice in turn and mix the juices together in a glass. Garnish with a slice of lemon.

Mango and Ginger Lassi

Lassis are Indian drinks, made with innumerable combinations of fresh yogurt and fruit or herbs. They are extremely refreshing, as well as being delicious and good for you.

Ingredients

1 mango

5 fl oz (150 ml) plain yogurt.

¾ in (2 cm) ginger

Method

Cut the mango in half and remove the stone. Cut the flesh away from the skin and juice. Add the juice to the yogurt in a blender and whiz until smooth. If you want to sweeten it, mix in a trickle of organic honey.

Citrus Special

Harness the ultra-powerful cleansing powers of citric acid to blast impurities from your body.

Ingredients

1 lemon

2 limes

3 oranges

Method

Peel all the fruit and break into segments. Remember to retain as much pith as possible. Juice the fruits and combine the juices together in a glass.

Beetroot Booster

A vibrant purple mix that will provide a gentle start to the day.

Ingredients

2 carrots

Half a cucumber

Third of a beetroot

Method

Scrub the carrots and top and tail them. Roughly chop the cucumber and scrub the beetroot before chopping it into chunks. Juice the beetroot, followed by the carrot and then the cucumber. Combine the juices in a glass.

Green Apple Blast

Pep up the apple juice with this combination of watercress and parsley.

Ingredients

2 apples
4 oz (125 g) watercress
Handful of parsley

Method

Rinse the watercress and juice, followed by the parsley (reserving a sprig for decoration). Roughly chop the apples and juice. Mix the juices together in a glass.

Liver Livener

A great recipe for enhancing the immune system. Packed with beta-carotene and anti-carcinogenic substances, particularly in the beetroot, this will leave you feeling refreshed and cleansed.

Ingredients

3 carrots

Third of a beetroot

Method

Scrub the carrots and top and tail them. Scrub the beetroot before chopping it into chunks. Juice the beetroot, followed by the carrot and mix the juices together in a glass.

Jolly Green Giant

This substantial recipe produces a juice cocktail packed with reviving goodness.

Ingredients

3 stalks celery

4–5 leaves spinach

3 tomatoes

An eighth head white cabbage

3 sprigs dill

1 lemon

Method

Rinse the cabbage and spinach leaves and juice. Remove the leafy tops from the celery and juice. Chop the tomatoes in half and add them to the juicer. Peel the lemon and juice. Mix the juices together in a glass. Finely chop two sprigs of dill and sprinkle over the top. Use the remaining sprig for decoration.

Leafy Apple Launcher

This peppery, herby concoction is a light refreshing juice that will fill you with energy.

Ingredients

2 apples

5 oz (150 g) white grapes

1 oz (25 g) watercress or rocket

Handful fresh coriander

Juice of half a lime

Method

Roughly chop the apples and juice them. Rinse the grapes, discard the stems, and juice. Peel the lime and juice half of it, reserving a slice for decoration. Rinse the watercress (or rocket) and coriander and juice. Combine all the juice in a glass and decorate with a slice of lime.

Fennel and Cabbage Fusion

A beautifully colored juice. The strong flavor of the red cabbage (if not its color!) is tempered by the sweetness of the apples. Fennel is an excellent purifying agent.

Ingredients

3.5 oz (100 g)
red cabbage

Half a fennel bulb

2 apples

Half a lemon

Method

Roughly chop the cabbage and juice. Remove the stalk from the fennel and juice. Roughly chop the apples and juice them. Peel the lemon, reserve a slice for decoration, and juice half of it. Mix the juices together in a glass.

Pinemint Juice

This is a simple yet delicious combination.

Ingredients
One pineapple
4 sprigs fresh mint

Method

Remove the rind from the pineapple an
juice the flesh. Reserve a sprig of mint fo
decoration and finely chop the rest. Ad
ice to a glass, pour in the pineappl
juice, and stir in the chopped min

Green Oranges

A simple, yet powerful blend of cleansing citrus juice.

Ingredients

3 medium oranges
1 lime
Sprig of mint

Method

Peel the oranges and the lime and juice. Finely chop the mint and sprinkle on top of the juice.

Cranberry Grape Cocktail

The cranberries will ensure that this cleansing juice flushes out your system.

Ingredients

2 apples

3.5 oz (100 g) grapes

1.75 oz (50 g) cranberries

1 slice lemon

Method

Rinse the cranberries and add to the juicer.
Rinse the grapes, remove from the stalks and
juice. Roughly chop the apples and juice.
Mix the juices together in a glass and
decorate with a slice of lemon.

Grapefruit Smoothie

A substantial and refreshing smoothie.

Ingredients

Half a pineapple
1 grapefruit, peeled
2.5 fl oz (75 ml) plain
yogurt

Method

Peel the grapefruit, break into segments and
juice. Remove the skin from the pineapple, cut
away the woody core and juice the flesh. Add
the juices to a blender with the yogurt and whiz
until smooth.

Speckled Tomatoes

Another delicious herby drink. Parsley is an excellent restorative as it contains calcium, iron, and potassium. Add a dash of Worcestershire sauce for a little more "bite" if you prefer.

Ingredients

6 tomatoes
6 leaves fresh basil
8 sprigs fresh parsley

Method

Finely chop the basil and parsley and juice the tomatoes. Reserve a sprig of parsley for decoration and stir the chopped herbs into the tomato juice.

Ginger Orange

A simple but effective juice. Juiced oranges are so much more substantial than orange juice in cartons and this is quite a filling juice. Dilute with a little water if you want to lessen the effects of the fruit sugars.

Ingredients

4 medium oranges, peeled

¾ in (2 cm) fresh ginger

Method

Peel the oranges, retaining as much pith as possible. Juice three of them. Peel the ginger and roughly chop. Juice this, followed by the remaining orange, which will flush out the juicer. Stir the juices together in a glass.

Mango and Grape Cocktail

Red grapes contain a substance called resveratrol, a powerful anticarcinogenic They are also excellent gentle cleansers.

Ingredients
1 mango
5 oz (150 g) red grape.

Method

Cut the mango in half and ease out the stone. Remov the peel and add the flesh to the juicer. Rinse the grape and juice them. Mix the juices together in a glass

Watermelon and Honey Tonic

An amazing juice that refreshes, cleanses, and is rumored to have aphrodisiac properties.

Ingredients

Watermelon – about a quarter

2 limes

Clear honey to taste

Iced water to dilute

Method

Cut the rind off the water melon and juice the flesh (pits included). Peel the limes and juice. Mix the juices with iced water to taste and add a little honey if required.

Spiced Apple

This spicy and relaxing blend is reminiscent of warm wintry drinks.

Ingredients

3 apples

*¼ teaspoon cinnamon
(or half a cinnamon
stick)*

*¾ in (2 cm) slice
of ginger*

Method

*Roughly chop the apples and juice them,
followed by the ginger. Mix the juices in
a glass and whisk in the cinnamon.*

Apricot Mango Orangery

A symphony of pastel orange colors, with the heady fragrance
of spring flowers.

Ingredients

4 apricots

1 mango

1 orange

Method

emove the stones from the apricots and juice
em. Cut the mango in half and remove the
one. Peel off the rind and juice the flesh.
el the orange and juice. Combine the
ices in a glass.

Power Booster

A light purple cocktail that will slip down easily, leaving you relaxed and ready for bed.

Ingredients

2 apples

4 oz (100 g) white grapes

2 oz (50 g) beetroot

½ in (1 cm) slice of fresh ginger

Method

Roughly chop the apples and juice. Rinse the grapes and add to the juicer. Scrub the beetroot before chopping it into chunks. Juice the beetroot followed by the ginger and mix all the juices together in a glass.

Super Salad

Remember the soporific effect of lettuces? This is a perfect juice to relax you before bedtime.

Ingredients

3 large tomatoes, halved
Half a little gem lettuce
2 in (5 cm) cucumber
Small handful of parsley
Half a lemon

Method

Rinse the lettuce leaves and juice. Chop the tomatoes in half and add to the juicer, followed by the cucumber and parsley. Peel the lemon and juice half of it. Combine the juices in a tall glass and sip slowly.

Apple Glow

This is a mild, restorative drink that is good for the skin.

Ingredients
1 apple
Half a honeydew melo
4 oz (100 g) red grape
Half a lemon

Metho
Remove the skin and pits from the melon an
juice. Chop the apple to fit the juicer and rinse th
grapes. Peel the lemon. Juice everything and m
the juices in a tall glas

Melon Marvel

This is quite a substantial juice to end the day and will ward off any further hunger pangs.

Ingredients

Half a canteloupe melon

2 pears

¾ in (2 cm) piece of fresh ginger

Method

Remove the pits and skin from the melon. Chop up the pear and remove the woody stem. Peel the ginger and roughly chop. Juice the pears, ginger, and melon in that order. Mix the juices together in a glass.

Apple and Ginger Tea

The ginger infuses with the apple juice to make a wonderful, aromatic blend of scents. This tea will soothe body and soul, restoring good humor and good health.

Ingredients

3 apples

2 in (5 cm) root ginger

5 fl oz (150 ml) water

Serves 1

Method

Juice the apples and finely slic the ginger. Add the mix to saucepan with 5 fl oz (150 m of water and bring to the boi Allow to simmer gently fc 15 minutes Strain, and pou into a cup

Mint Tea

Mint makes a refreshing tea that helps soothe the digestive system. It is especially popular in North Africa, where brewing and consuming it has evolved as an art form, only slightly less ritualized than the Japanese tea ceremony. There are a number of recipes, but this one seems to be a reasonably popular version.

Ingredients

large bunch fresh mint

2 pints (1 liter) water

desert spoon of sugar (or to taste)

Serves 4 (approximately)

Method

pour the boiling water over the mint and simmer for 15 minutes. train and pour into cups. dd sugar to taste.

Lemon and Mint Tea

This refreshing blend can be drunk hot or cold. As a hot drink, it is very soothing for colds, while on a hot day, it is extremely refreshing served cold and poured over ice.

Ingredients

1 lemon

1 tablespoon finely chopped mint leaves

7 fl oz (200 ml) water

Serves 1

Method

Using a lemon zester, scrape th aromatic rind off the lemon. Mix wit the mint leaves in a tea diffuser an dangle in a mug of boiling water. C simmer the water, lemon, and mint in saucepan. Leave to infuse for at lea five minutes, strain, and pour into mug

Parsley Tea

Parsley is valued for its diuretic action and parsley tea is an old folk remedy used to aid digestion. As it helps eliminate uric acid, it can help those who suffer from gout or rheumatism. It is rich in chlorophyl, calcium, iron, and vitamins A and C, so if you really want a tea that is good for you, brew a pot of parsley.

Ingredients

Large bunch of fresh parsley

7 fl oz (200 ml) boiling water

Method

To make one cup, finely chop a medium-sized bunch – you need enough for a tablespoon of finely chopped herb. Add the parsley to a tea diffuser, suspend it over a mug and pour on boiling water. Leave to brew for at least five minutes and then drink, adding a squeeze of lemon to taste.

Ginger Tea

Ginger tea fills a kitchen with the most wonderful warm spicy aroma. It produces a refreshing tea that is particularly delicious on cold days.

Ingredients

4 in (10 cm) thinly sliced fresh ginger (peeled)

2 pints (1 liter)water

2 tablespoons honey or brown sugar

Lemon wedges for garnish if desired

Makes 4 cups

Method

Peel the ginger and cut into thin slices. Simmer the ginger and water together for at least 20 minutes – longer for stronger tea. Add the honey or sugar and strain the tea through a sieve set over a teapot. Serve garnished with lemon wedges or slices of ginger.

Iced Lemon & Ginger Tea

Lemon and ginger are a combination of flavors made in heaven.

Ingredients

4 in (10 cm) piece
fresh ginger

2 pints (1 liter) water

2 oz (50 g) honey

2 oz (50 g) sugar

Zest of 2 lemons, removed with a
vegetable peeler or lemon zester

Juice of four lemons

Garnish: lemon slices

Method

*Peel the ginger and cut into thin slices. In a medium
saucepan boil the water, ginger, honey, sugar, and zest,
stirring until the sugar is dissolved. Remove the pan
from the heat and allow the tea to infuse covered for
45 minutes. Uncover the tea and cool completely.*

Junior Juices

Most of the book extolled the virtues of healthy eating and has emphasized the damage done to our health by convenience food, but this chapter changes tack slightly. Smoothies and milk shakes are delicious and usually nutritious additions to any diet. They are particularly quick and easy to prepare, requiring little more than roughly chopping the fruity ingredients and adding them to a blender or food processor with milk, coconut cream, or ice cream. The ingredients are endlessly versatile, so smoothies can be consumed at any time of day. They are especially popular with children, particularly if ice cream is involved.

Kids love cooking: from the messy preparatory stages to the licking of the bowl and the consumption of the finished product, it's all great fun. What many of them do not like, however, is anything that looks remotely green or healthy, and as they get older, the peer pressure to conform and have lunch boxes filled with junk food becomes greater. If you ban children from eating a particularly desirable e-number infested, sugar-encrusted confection, the allure of it will grow stronger. Remember the old adage of "a little of what you fancy does you good" and, in the case of cookies and candies, a moderate intake will do no harm, as long as the rest of the child's diet is well-balanced. Try matching the unhealthy with the healthy by giving the kids a juicy treat after school.

This is all leading up to a chapter on juices for children. Vegetables are few and far between, and yogurt and ice

Spotty smoothie. See page 191

ream are included to make shakes and
moothies. Even chocolate can be
ncorporated as part of a health-giving
rink. Nutritionists agree that children
eed sugar and fats to ensure healthy
rowth, so give them a treat! The fruit
uices will still impart most of their magic
ven if they are adulterated with a little
e cream on high days and holidays.

You might like to try introducing a
outine of fresh juice after school, when
any children return home dehydrated
nd low on blood sugar. A blast of fresh
uice will restore their blood sugar levels
along with their good humor) and keep
em going till tea time. And you can be
ertain that even if they sneaked off to
e candy shop on the way home, or
wapped their wholemeal sandwiches for
hips at lunchtime, they have consumed
least one healthy item!

Juices are a terrific addition to a child's
iet, but if you are worried about your
ild's food intake and overall health
onsult a doctor.

Equipment

A blender is vital to make really smooth
smoothies. If you are approaching this
chapter from the point of view of fun
rather than health, or if time and space
are pressing, blend all the ingredients
together from the start, rather than
juicing the fruit and then adding it to the
blender. True, the smoothies will not be
quite so packed full of vitamins, but the
fiber will be incorporated and the drinks
will still taste fantastic.

Ice

Crushed ice creates long, cold drinks, or
even slushies. Ice and blenders are not
always a perfect combination. Some
blenders are simply not strong enough to
deal with rock-solid ice cubes, Do not
add whole ice cubes to your blender
unless you are sure it is powerful enough
to cope with them. Wrap about ten ice
cubes in a clean tea towel and bash them
with a hammer or meat mallet before
adding them to the blender. Or use a

proprietary ice crusher, which is a useful and reasonably cheap addition to your kitchen utensils.

Make flavored crushed ice by mixing your favourite juice with crushed ice and re-freezing it just long enough for the juice to freeze, but not long enough for it all to become a solid block. (See the slushie section on page 186.)

Straws and cocktail umbrellas – you can't have too many.

Color adds to the whole experience of making smoothies – the brighter and more vibrant, the better. Packets of frozen berries are really useful here: not only do they produce deep purple and garish pink drinks, but they rattle around the blender in an extremely satisfying manner, too.

Glasses

If children are participating, use robust glasses or invest in some fancy plastic picnic glasses to spare yourself the pain, danger, and nuisance of breakage. Kids love zany colored plastic beakers, but they will hide the natural colors of the juices and smoothies. In all honesty, most children are less concerned with the aesthetic aspect of juicing than the taste and quantity, so chose glasses that are sturdy and stable – and dishwasher proof if you have one.

One useful disposable receptacle is a pineapple shell. It is exceptionally easy to produce one if you use a pineapple corer which twists down through the pineapple, removing the flesh as pineapple rings and leaving the core and shell intact. Simply chop out most of the core, and use the shell as a tropical glass – no washing-up required!

Similarly, coconut shells add a touch of *The Jungle Book* to a kids' juicing session. Bang a hole in the top of a coconut, pour off the milk (and use it with pineapple for a great smoothie), and saw off the top of the shell. Voilà – a sturdy tropical drinking vessel!

Top tips for super smoothies

- Save time – simply add all the ingredients to a blender rather than juicing the fruit first and then blending it.

- Chop up the ingredients to a roughly similar size before adding to the blender; if they are smaller than a golf ball the blender will be able to process them more easily.

- Give the mixture a short, sharp burst on full power for 20–30 seconds, then open the lid to check that nothing is stuck under the blender blade.

- Add ice cubes gradually, two or three at a time and blend until the ice cubes have stopped jiggling around the blender. If your blender is not strong enough to deal with ice cubes, add a little water to the mixture to give it the consistency of a milkshake.

- Add more fruit or yogurt to make a thick smoothie.

- Use frozen fruit (especially berries) for intensely flavored, icy drinks.

The quantities in this chapter are sometimes slightly smaller to take into account the smaller appetites of children. Double up the recipes if they need more, or if you're making them for big kids!

Slushies

Slushies are long, cold drinks made with crushed ice, fruit juice, and sometimes concentrated cordial. They can be imbibed through a long, wide straw, which concentrates their intensely fruity flavor. Flavored slushies can be made by partially freezing fresh fruit juice and water, and stirring it all up before it becomes frozen solid.

Basic slushie mixes

Use enough fruit to make about 7 fl oz (200 ml) of juice and mix with about 3.5 fl oz (100 ml) of water. Citrus fruits and berries make the best slushie mixes, but remember that the amount of juice extracted depends on the type of juicer you use. Aim to use about four oranges, or one and a half grapefruit, six limes, one pineapple, 10 oz (275 g) strawberries or raspberries. Melon juice also works well, but it is naturally quite watery, so leave out the water; one honeydew melon will make enough for the recipes below, or half a watermelon.

Method

Juice the oranges and mix with the water in a shallow container and put it in the freezer for an hour. Remove from the freezer and stir the crystals around. Return to the freezer for another half hour and then stir the ice around. It is now ready to use.

Fizzies

Fresh juice mixed with a commercial fizz may be a bit of a cop-out, but these recipes all offer an unusual combination of flavors and sensations that you will want to mix again and again. They're extremely quick and easy to concoct and are ideal if you are having a party and need interesting drinks for those averse to alcohol. The drinks at the end of this section may be more popular with adults than children simply because they are not quite so sweet!

Strawberry Smoothie

Containing three firm children's favorites.

Ingredients

5 oz (150 g)
strawberries

1 banana

1 orange

Method

Wipe the strawberries, and hull them. Peel the banana and chop into chunks. Peel the orange and break into segments. Put the whole lot into a blender and whiz until creamy. Add ice or a little freshly squeezed orange juice to dilute if desired.

Mango Madness

This is an excellent way to introduce children to the subtle flavors of mangos.

Ingredients

3 oranges
Half a ripe banana
Half a mango
Serves 2

Method

Peel the oranges and the banana. Cut the
stone out of the mango and scoop the flesh
into the blender. Add the bananas and
oranges. Whiz until smooth. Dilute with a
little chilled water if it appears too thick.
Pour into a tall glass

Top of the Morning Smoothie

Those who are suspicious of vegetables may turn up their small noses at this drink, but if they can be persuaded to taste it, they are sure to enjoy it. It contains strawberries, so it can't be all bad!

Ingredients

2 oranges

2 carrots

1 apple, 1 mango

6 strawberries

Ice cubes and slices of orange to decorate

5 fl oz (150 ml) plain yogurt

(Serves 2–3)

Method

Top and tail the carrots and add to the juicer. Pour the juice into the blender. Peel and core the apple and chop into chunks. Remove the stone from the mango and add the pulp to the blender. Peel the oranges, break into segments and add them to the blender along with the chopped apple and the strawberries. Blend until smooth, then add the ice, a few cubes at a time. Add the yogurt and whiz until the mixture is thick and creamy.

Apricot Smoothie

This delicately colored smoothie is both sophisticated and delicious.

Ingredients

5 apricots

3 oranges

2.5 fl oz (75 ml) yogurt

Serves 1

Method

Peel the apricots and remove the stones. Peel the oranges and break into chunks. Add the fruit to the blender and whiz until smooth. Add the yogurt and blend again.

Spotty Smoothie

Raspberry and oranges are a wonderful combination, but the raspberry pips refuse to be juiced or blended and suspend themselves in the smoothie.

Ingredients

4 oz (125 g) raspberries

2 oranges

2.5 fl oz (75 ml) plain yogurt

Method

Peel the oranges and break into segments. Rinse the raspberries and juice them, followed by the oranges. Add the juices to a blender with the yogurt and whiz until smooth. Alternatively, add the fruits to the blender and whiz until smooth, then add the yogurt. Dilute with a little water if needed.

Berry Smoothie

This is a beautiful purple color. The addition of the blackcurrant squash makes the flavor a little less tart for those with a sweet tooth.

Ingredients

5 oz (150 g) blackcurrants

5 oz (150 g) yogurt

2 tsp blackcurrant syrup (or squash)

4 fl oz (100 ml) milk (optional)

Method

Rinse the blackcurrants and remove them from the stems. Add to the blender with the yogurt, milk and blackcurrant syrup. Whiz until smooth and purple. Decorate with a sprig of blackcurrants.

Strawberry Yogurt Smoothie

Delicious, filling and extremely quick to make!

Ingredients

5 fl oz (150 ml)
strawberry yogurt

1 banana

2 oranges

Method

Peel the oranges and break into segments.
Peel the banana. Add everything to the
blender and whiz until smooth. Reserve a
slice of orange or a strawberry for
decoration.

Peach, Banana and Pineapple Smoothie

A summery drink with a hint of the tropics.

Ingredients

2 peaches

1 banana

Half a pineapple

2.5 fl oz (75 ml) yogur

Serves 2

Metho

Remove the skin from the pineapple an
chop the flesh into chunks. Remove th
stones from the peaches and slice int
quarters. Peel the banana and chop in
chunks. Add all the fruit to the blender an
whiz for 30 seconds or until smooth (you migl
need to add a little water). Add the yogurt an
whiz until smooth

Chocolate Bananas

An irresistible combination that will appeal to chocolate lovers everywhere.

Ingredients

2 bananas

1 orange

2.5 fl oz (75 ml) yogurt

Grated chocolate

Method

Peel the bananas and orange and blend briefly. Add the yogurt and blend again. If the mixture seems too thick, either add a little more orange juice, or a shot of milk. Pour into a tall glass and decorate with lots of grated chocolate.

Banana and Pineapple

Tangy, refreshing and filling – the perfect juice to serve up after school to revive starving children.

Ingredients

1 banana

Half a pineapple

2 fl oz (50 ml) orange juice

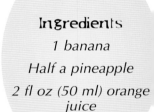

Method

Peel the banana and chop into chunks. Cut the pineapple in half, remove the core and the skin and chop the flesh into chunks. Add to the blender with the banana and orange juice and whiz until smooth.

Ice Cream Bananas

This is more of a milk shake, but satisfaction is guaranteed.

Ingredients

2 ripe bananas

1 scoop chocolate ice cream

4 fl oz (100 ml) milk

Method

Peel the bananas and add all the ingredients to a blender. Whiz until thick and creamy. Drink through a straw and lap up the remaining bits with a spoon!

Raspberry Ripple

An old favourite, but once made with fresh raspberries, shop-bought raspberry ripple will never pass your lips again.

Ingredients

5 oz (150 g) raspberries

2 scoops vanilla ice cream

Method

Add the raspberries and one scoop of ice cream to a blender. Place the other scoop in a glass. Pour the creamy mixture over the single scoop. Pause to admire your handiwork briefly, then enjoy.

Tropical Ambrosia

A heady mix of coconut and pineapple. It will smell like a Pina Colada, but without the alcoholic punch.

Ingredients

Half a pineapple

1 apple

2–3 tablespoons coconut milk

1 orange

1 banana

Serves 2

Method

Peel the banana and orange, remove the pineapple skin and chop the flesh into chunks, then chop the apple into chunks. Juice the apple, orange and pineapple and pour the juices into the blender. Add the banana and coconut milk and whiz until smooth. Serve in a tall glass decorated with a cocktail umbrella and small chunk of pineapple on a cocktail stick.

Banana Berries

This is made most easily by throwing everything in the blender and whizzing until smooth.

Ingredients

7 oz (200 g) cranberrie

1 banana

1 lime

2 oranges

Serve 2

Method

Rinse the cranberries, peel the banana and chop into chunks. Peel the lime and the oranges and break into segments. Add the oranges and lime to the blender and whiz briefly. Then add the cranberries, whiz, and then add the banana. If the mixture is too thick for the blender, add a little water to dilute it

Aloha Hawaii

The fruits of a tropical island, combined with a hint of coconut milk to remind you that the surf's up! Use a pineapple corer to deal with the pineapple, and drink this juice out of the shell, garnished with a couple of cocktail umbrellas.

Ingredients

1 grapefruit

2 oranges

1 pineapple

4 fl oz (100 ml) coconut milk

Serves 2

Method

This is another recipe that can be tackled by the blender alone. Peel the oranges and the grapefruit and break into segments. Chop up the pineapple, removing the skin and the core. Blend the citrus fruits first, then add the pineapple and finally the coconut milk, giving the blender a good whiz to make everything thick and creamy.

Peachy Pineapple Fling

The smooth peach juice enhances the zing of the pineapple and lime juice.

Ingredients

3 peaches

1 lime

1 pineapple

Method

Remove the stones from the peaches, chop to fit
the juicer. Chop the pineapple into four, remove
the skin and chop the flesh to fit the juicer (reserve
a couple of small chunks for decoration). Peel the
lime and cut in half. Juice the peaches,
pineapple, and lime, and pour the juices into two
glasses. Decorate with straws and pineapple
chunks on cocktail sticks.

Pineapple and Orange

This simple combination of orange and pineapple looks absolutely
delicious and tastes even better.

Ingredients

Half a pineapple

*Orange slushie mixture
(see page 186)*

Serves 2

Method

*Prepare the slushie mixture as on page 186.
Remove the skin from the pineapple and
juice the flesh. Divide the slushie mixture
between two glasses and drizzle the
pineapple juice over the ice crystals.*

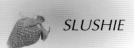

Strawberry and Peach

Peaches and strawberries are a wonderful summery combination. Make this to enjoy on a warm day.

Ingredients

3 peaches

1 quantity strawberry slushie mix (see page 186)

Serves 2

Method

Prepare the strawberry slushie mixture (see page 186) and divide it between two glasses. Cut the peaches into quarters and remove the stones. Add to the juicer and pour the juice over the strawberry slushie. Serve with straws and cocktail umbrellas.

Frozen Melon

Melons are extremely watery fruits, and so produce large amounts of juice. This blend of melon and icy orange makes a delicious long drink.

Ingredients

Half a canteloupe melon

1 quantity orange slushie mix (see page 186)

Serves 2

Method

Prepare the orange slushie mix a couple of hours before you want to serve the drink. Remove the seeds from the melon and scoop the flesh out of the skin. Juice the melon. Divide the orange slushie between two glasses and pour on the melon juice.

Peach Slushie

This delicately flavored, yet robust slushie will make a satisfying snack.

Ingredients

2 frozen peaches skin
removed

5 fl oz (150 ml) peach
yogurt

About 10 ice cubes

Method

Cut the peach into quarters and remove the ski
and the stone. Freeze for a couple of hours a
least. When you are ready to make the slushie
add the peach quarters to the blender alon
with the yogurt. Process until smooth, and the
add the ice cubes a few at a time, processing i
short bursts until they are incorporated

Orange Blossom

The wonderful aroma of fresh oranges and nectarine conjures up visions of blossom-filled gardens.

Ingredients

2 oranges

2 nectarines

2.5 fl oz (75 ml) plain yogurt

About 10 ice cubes

Method

Cut the nectarines into quarters and remove the skin and the stone. Peel the oranges and break into segments. Add the nectarine quarters to the blender along with the oranges and the yogurt juice. Process until smooth, and then add the ice cubes a few at a time, processing in short bursts until they are incorporated.

Green Snow

It may be the color of slime, but this slushie has an almost floral flavor. The melon combines with the kiwi fruit to produce a delicious pick-me-up.

Ingredients

3 kiwis

1 quantity of melon slushie (see page 186)

Serves 2

Method

Peel the kiwi fruit and juice them. Stir the juice into the melon slush and watch it turn an extraordinary shade of pale green

Frozen Barbie

A gorgeous pink drink, which even the toughest kid will enjoy,
in spite of the color.

Ingredients

*Strawberry slushie mix
(see page 186)*

Half a watermelon

Serves 2

Method

*Remove the rind from the watermelon and
chop into chunks to fit the juicer. Don't
worry about the pits – the juicer will cope
with them. Stir the juice into the frozen
strawberry mixture.*

Muddy River

This tastes far better than it sounds – honest!

Ingredients

4 fl oz (100 ml) orange juice – juice of two oranges

4 fl oz (100 ml) cola

Ice cubes

Method

Peel the oranges and juice them. Add a few ice cubes to a glass and pour the orange juice in. Mix with the cola for a fizzy and unusual taste sensation

Green Slime

This drink oozes goodness, despite the fact that the color matches the damp green of Shrek the ogre's skin.

Ingredients

3 kiwis

4 fl oz (100 ml) carbonated lemonade or soda water

Method

Peel the kiwis and juice them. Add a few ice cubes to a glass and pour the kiwi juice in. Stir in the lemonade or soda water, pop in a couple of straws, and slurp!

Coke Float

Sounds disgusting? Try it and you'll be hooked. It's extremely satisfying to make, as the combination of cola and ice cream verges on the combustible and fizzes very satisfyingly.

Ingredients

7 fl oz (200 ml) cola

1 scoop vanilla ice cream

2 oz (50 g) strawberries

Method

Rinse the strawberries and whiz them in the blender until they're thick. Pour the cola into a glass and carefully float the ice cream on top. Drizzle a little of the strawberry juice over the ice cream and watch it merge into the froth.

Peach and Orange Fizz

The peach juice tones down the acidic tartness of the orange to make
an almost subtle fizz.

Ingredients

2 peaches

1 orange

4 fl oz (100 ml)
sparkling water

Method

*Remove the stone from the peaches and
juice. Peel the orange and juice it, then mix
the juice with the peach juice and sparkling
water. Serve with a couple of straws.*

Hurricane Blaster

This is a refreshing drink ideal for cooling down hot children (or adults, actually). Make some and hand it out before they start demanding cola.

Ingredients

Half a pineapple

2 apples

Soda water or sparkling water to taste

Method

Remove the skin from the pineapple and chop the flesh into chunks. Chop the apple and add to the juicer, followed by the pineapple. Mix the juices with approximately 2–4 fl oz (50–100 ml) of sparkling water in a tall glass.

Pink Lemonade

This is probably what Barbie drinks in her more sophisticated moments.

Ingredients

*8 oz (225 g)
strawberries*

*4 fl oz (100 ml)
lemonade*

Method

*Wash and hull the strawberries, reserving one
for decoration. Add the strawberries to the blender
and whiz until blended, add the lemonade and whiz
carefully, making sure that the carbon dioxide does not
cause the whole lot to fizz over. Slice the remaining
strawberry thinly and float on top of the drink.
This looks most effective served in wide
cocktail glasses.*

Sparkling Orange Lime Juice

Fizzy orange is a great drink, but the addition of the limes makes the flavor a little more interesting.

Ingredients

2 oranges

1 lime

*4 fl oz (100 ml)
sparkling water or
lemonade*

Method

Peel the oranges and the lime, break into segments and juice. Pour the juice onto some ice cubes and mix with either lemonade or sparkling water.

Little Buck's Fizz

This delicious juice looks quite sophisticated and might be nice served as a celebratory drink, or when adults are having champagne.

Ingredients

5 oz (150 g) grapes

Half a lemon

2 oranges

Sparkling mineral water and ice

Serves two

Method

Peel the oranges and break into quarters to fit the juicer. Reserve a couple of slices of lemon for garnish, and peel the rest. Rinse the grapes, remove from the stalks and juice. Juice the oranges, followed by the lemon half. Pour the juices into two glasses, add ice and top up with sparkling mineral water.

Mango Lemon Cooler

A thirst-quenching blend of juices to add fizz to your kids (as if they need it!)

Ingredients

1 mango

Half a lemon

Sparkling mineral water and crushed ice.

Garnish with a slice of lemon.

Serves 2

Method

Cut the mango in half and remove the stone. Cut off the rind and juice the flesh. Peel the lemon, reserving a slice for garnish. Juice half the lemon and mix the juice with the mango juice. Pour into two glasses and top up with sparkling water.

Highland Fling

It seems amazing that the most jewel-like, luscious raspberries are often the product of the chilly countryside of northern Europe.

Ingredients

9 oz (250 g) raspberries

1 lemon

4 fl oz (100 ml) sparkling water

Serves 2

Method

Reserve two slices of the lemon for decoration and peel the rest. Rinse the raspberries and juice them, followed by the lemon. Mix the juices together in a glass and top up with sparkling water. Garnish with the lemon slices and maybe a few raspberries.

Strawberry Surprise

Decorate with small fruit kebab of strawberry and lemon slice on a cocktail stick

Ingredients

7 oz (200 g) strawberries

2 apples

4 fl oz (100 ml) sparkling water or lemonade

Method

Rinse the strawberries and add to the juicer. Roughly chop the apples and juice. Mix the juices in a glass and top up with the carbonated liquid of your choice. Decorate with fruit kebabs and straws

Grapefruit Fizz

The apple tones the acidity of the grapefruit, which may be too tart for children's taste buds.

Ingredients

1 grapefruit

1 apple

4 fl oz (100 ml)
sparkling water

Method

Peel the grapefruit and break into segments. Roughly chop the apple. Juice the apple and then the grapefruit. Divide the juice between two glasses and top up with sparkling water.

Lizzie's Lovely Lime Fizz

The lime modifies the sweetness of the cola and makes a pleasantly refreshing drink.

Ingredients
2 limes
4 fl oz (150 ml) cola
Ice cubes

Method
Peel the limes and juice them. Pour the juice into a glass and add two or three ice cubes. Top up with cola. Add a straw and slurp!

Juice to Go

If the chapters on health and detoxification have depressed you, try some of the juices in this chapter, hedonistic drinks all. Some of these recipes grew out of the drinks in the Junior Juice chapter and have been altered for the more sophisticated adult palate. (If you're in need of smoothies, however, see pages 187–202). Others are based on popular cocktails, but lack the alcohol. All of them are meant to be enjoyed and the fact that they are good for you is merely secondary. Make them at the weekend when you probably have a little more time to potter around the kitchen and experiment. They are also great for parties and will provide the non-drinkers with something a little more inspiring than cola or plain old soda water.

Captain Cook's Cocktail

The great explorer, Captain Cook, eliminated scurvy among his sailors by administering lime juice to each of them every day. He would probably approve of this. It is the most refreshing juice in the book, especially on a hot day. Make lots, and earn popularity points among family and friends.

Ingredients

4 limes

4 fl oz (100 ml) sparkling water

Crushed ice

Sugar to taste

Serves 2

Method

Peel the limes and juice them. Crush few ice cubes and add to a glass. Pour the lime juice on top and top up with sparkling water. Stir in a little sugar to taste if desired.

Pear Drop

As well as being terrifically full of anti-inflammatory phytonutrients, this juice is a heady reminder of the candy store.

Ingredients

3 pears

4 oz (100 g)
blackcurrants

Crushed ice

Method

Rinse the blackcurrants and juice. Chop the woody stalk off the pears and juice them. Crush about five ice cubes and add to a glass. Pour the juices over the ice and stir with a swizzle stick.

Lemon, Lime and Ginger

An excellent non-alcoholic drink to serve to the non-drinkers at parties.

Ingredients

7 fl oz (200 ml) ginger ale

Half a lemon

2 limes

Ice

Method

Peel the lemon and limes and juice. Pour the juice into a tall glass, add some ice cubes and top up with ginger ale.

Pina Colada

Far from being a pale imitation of the real thing, this is a fresh and tangy cocktail, sometimes known as a Virgin Colada because it lacks rum.

Ingredients

1 pineapple

4 fl oz (100 ml) coconut milk

Crushed ice

Serves 2

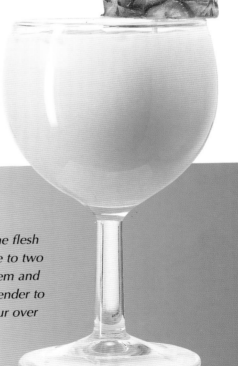

Method

Remove the skin from the pineapple and cut the flesh into chunks. Add to the juicer. Add crushed ice to two glasses, divide the pineapple juice between them and stir in the coconut milk. Alternatively, use a blender to blend the pineapple and coconut milk and pour over crushed ice.

Gingered Apple Juice

Spice up some freshly juiced apples with fresh ginger.

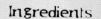

Ingredients

2 apples

*4 fl oz (100 ml)
ginger ale*

Slice of lemon

Method

*Chop the apples and add to the juicer. Mix the
juice with the ginger ale in a tall glass and decorate
with a cocktail umbrella and a slice of lemon.*

Cranberry and Ginger Spritzer

This is not quite as dry as a sea breeze, but is equally refreshing.

Ingredients

9 oz (250 g) cranberries

2 apples

7 fl oz (200 ml) chilled ginger ale

crushed ice

Method

Juice the cranberries and then the apples. Add the crushed ice to a jug and pour in the fruit juices. Add the ginger ale, stir, and serve. Float a few cranberries on top for decoration.

Virgin Mary

A Bloody Mary is a classic cocktail usually made with vodka. Remove the vodka, and you have an upliftingly virtuous and appetizing juice.

Ingredients

6 tomatoes

Dash of Tabasco

Dash of Worcestershire sauce

Half a lemon

2 sticks of celery

Method

Chop the tomatoes in half and peel the lemon juice. Juice the tomatoes, followed by half the lemon and one stick of celery. Mix the juices together in a tall glass, adding a couple of drops of Worcestershire sauce and Tabasco. Stir well and garnish with the remaining stick of celery.

The Gardener

Reward the gardener in the family with this hearty juice. Serve it after a hard day's pruning, planting, mowing, or weeding, and you may be forgiven for not helping!

Ingredients

4 carrots

1 celery stick

1 melon

Serves 4

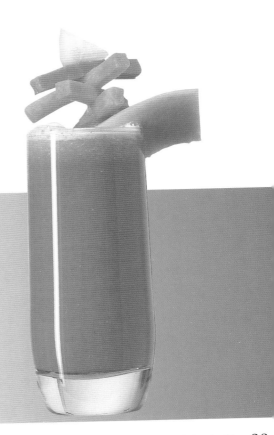

Method

Top and tail the carrots. Chop the melon into quarters and remove the pits. Cut off the rind and roughly chop the flesh. Juice the carrots, followed by the celery and then the melon. Add the juices to a jug and stir.

Orchard Melon

A juice to imbibe while contemplating apple trees laden with fruit.

Ingredients

Half a yellow or cantaloupe melon

1 apple

Fizzy water

Method

Remove the pits and rind from the melon and add the flesh to the juicer. Juice the apple and combine the juices in a tall glass, topping it up with sparkling mineral water.

Harvest Fruit

Based on the abundance of a September orchard, this works best with juicy King William pears.

Ingredients

4 apricots

4 plums

2 pears

Half a teaspoon cinnamon

Half a lemon

Method

Chop the apricots and plums in half and remove the stones. Cut the pears into quarters, removing the woody stalks. Peel the lemon. Reserve a small chunk of each fruit and make a decorative fruit kebab by spearing them on a cocktail stick. Juice the apricot, followed by the plums, the pear, and finally half the lemon. Mix the juices together in a glass with the cinnamon, and garnish with the fruit kebab.

Crabapple Fling

This fruity combination is as refreshing as it is colorful and is a perfect pick-me-up at any time of day.

Ingredients

7 oz (200g) cranberries

1 apple

1 lime

Sparkling water
(optional)

Method

Rinse the cranberries and juice them. Chop the apple and peel the lime. Juice both and mix all the juices together in a glass. Add ice and top up with sparkling water if desired.

St Clements

The classic Cockney cooler, its name originates with the nursery rhyme,
'Oranges and lemons go the bells of Saint Clements.'

Ingredients

3 oranges

1 lemon

Sparkling mineral water
or lemonade

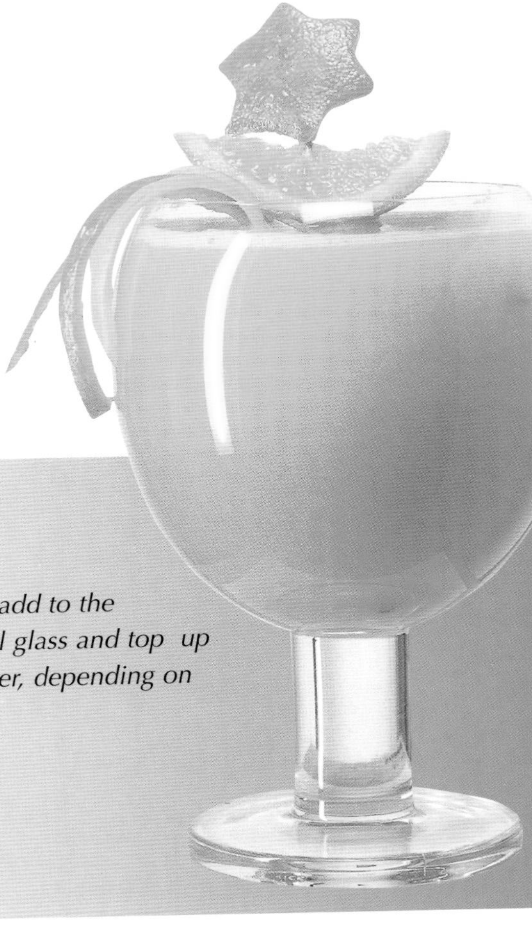

Method

*Peel the oranges and the lemon and add to the
juicer. Stir the juices together in a tall glass and top up
with either lemonade or mineral water, depending on
your taste.*

Strawberry Breeze

A great mix of flavors, with the sweetness of the strawberry overlaid by the slightly more tart lime and cranberry.

Ingredients

5 oz (150 g) cranberries

5 oz (150 g) strawberries

1 lime

Method

Rinse the berries and peel the lime. Reserve a couple of cranberries for decoration. Juice the cranberries, followed by the strawberries and the lime. Stir the juices together in a glass and garnish with a couple of cranberries.

Pacific Cocktail

Lie back, sip your juice and allow yourself to be transported to the South Pacific.

Ingredients

Half a pineapple

Half a lime

7 fl oz (200 ml) dry ginger ale

Two teaspoons of grenadine

Serves 2

Method

Chop up the pineapple, remove the skin and add to the juicer. Reserve a slice of lime for garnish and peel the rest before adding it to the juicer. Add some ice cubes to a jug, pour in the juices add the grenadine and ginger ale and stir.

Grapefruit Fizz

This juice has masses of natural zing. Tone down the citric tartness by mixing with lemonade rather than sparkling water if you prefer.

Ingredients

1 grapefruit

1 lime

Mineral water or lemonade

Ice cubes

Method

Peel the grapefruit and the lime (reserve a slice of lime for decoration) and juice. Pour the juices over some ice cubes in a glass and top up with the mineral water or lemonade.

Grape Cooler

A great color and a lovely, dry taste.

Ingredients

*4 oz (100 g)
red grapes*

7 oz (200 g) cranberries

1 lime

Sparkling mineral water

Ice cubes

Method

Peel the lime (reserve a slice of lime for decoration) and juice. Reserve a couple of strawberries and cranberries for decoration and juice the rest. Pour the juices over some ice cubes in a glass and top up with the mineral water. Spear the grapes, cranberries and slice of lime on a cocktail stick to decorate.

Flamingo

Take flight with this delicately colored juice. The sweetness of the raspberries and pineapple are offset by the tang of lemon juice.

Ingredients
7 oz (200 g) raspberries
Half a pineapple
1 lemon
Sparkling mineral water
Ice cubes
Serves two

Method
Cut the rind off the pineapple and add the flesh to the juicer. Juice the raspberries. Reserve two slices of lemon, peel the rest and juice it. Crush some ice and divide between two glasses. Pour in the juices, top up with mineral water and stir.

Prohibition Punch

This zesty juice is based on a recipe from the Prohibition era, when alcohol was outlawed.

Ingredients

2 oranges

3 apples

1 lemon

4 fl oz (100 ml) ginger ale

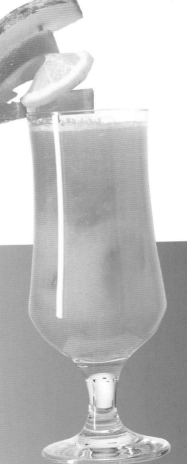

Method

Peel the oranges and the lemon and juice them.
Chop up the apples to fit the juicer and juice.
Add some ice cubes to a glass, pour in the juices,
stir and top up with ginger ale.

Green Ice

This intensely colored juice is wonderful on a hot summer's day.

Ingredients
3 kiwis
1 apple
Sprig of mint
Crushed ice

Method
Chop the kiwis and the apple to fit the blender. Crush about five ice cubes. Pour the juices over the crushed ice and decorate with a sprig of mint.

Tail Feathers

This juice is based on the Highball popular during Prohibition.

Ingredients

3 oranges

2 limes

1 sprig mint (about 10 leaves)

4 fl oz (100 ml) ginger ale

Crushed ice

Method

Reserve half the mint leaves and juice the rest. Peel the oranges and the limes and juice them. Crush two or three ice cubes and pour the juices over it. Top up with ginger ale. Decorate with the tail feathers – the sprig of mint.

Virgin Bellini

Reminiscent of a real Bellini cocktail (peach juice and champagne),
but without the alcohol.

Ingredients

2 peaches

1 orange

1 teaspoon grenadine

Half a lemon

*4 fl oz (100 ml)
sparkling mineral
water*

Method

*Cut the peaches in half, remove the stones and juice.
Peel the oranges and lemon and juice. Add some ice
cubes to a glass, pour over the grenadine and add the
juices. Stir, and top up with mineral water.*

Lettuce Lounge Lizard

Although lettuce juice is bitter, it is extremely good for you. Mask the flavor by mixing it with sweeter ingredients and drink in the essential nutrients.

Ingredients

Lettuce – 5 large leaves
3 apples
2 tangerines
Half a lemon

Method

Rinse the lettuce leaves and roughly chop the apples. Peel the tangerines and the lemon. Juice the lettuce, apples, tangerines and lemon and mix the juices together in a glass.

Coriander Pair

Spice up the mild taste of pear and carrot with a handful of coriander, which will help improve your circulation.

Ingredients

2 pears

2 carrots

Coriander – small handful

Method

Top and tail the carrots, scrub them and juice. Finely chop the coriander, reserving a sprig for garnish. Cut the woody stalks off the pears and juice. Mix the juices together and stir in the coriander.

Celery Cuke

An appealing combination of flavors, this juice, which is packed with vitamin C, also offers excellent protection against colds and tonsillitis. The bromelain in the pineapple helps heal the lining of a mouth made sore by coughs or a sore throat.

Ingredients

3 inches (7 cm) cucumber

Half a pineapple

2 carrots

3 sticks celery

Serves 2

Method

Scrub the carrots and top and tail them. Chop the cucumber into chunks to fit the juicer. Cut the rind off the pineapple. Juice the carrots, one stick of celery, pineapple, and cucumber. Mix the juices together in a jug and then pour into two glasses. Garnish with the remaining sticks of celery.

The Fawlty Towers

Aromatic basil lends a fragrant air to this vegetable juice. The irascible Mr Fawlty would have been a changed man if he had tried it.

Ingredients

3 tomatoes

Watercress – large handful

3 inches (7 cm) cucumber

Basil 5–7 leaves

1 stick celery

Method

Chop the tomatoes and cucumber to fit the juicer. Finely chop the basil. Juice the watercress, tomatoes, and cucumber. Pour the juices into a glass, sprinkle the chopped basil over the top and stir together with the celery (the tribute tower).

Ruby Apples

Use green apples to produce a colorful drink of contrasting hues.

Ingredients

2 apples

An eighth of a
watermelon
(approximately)

Method

*Roughly chop the apples and juice them. Remove
the skin from the watermelon and juice. Stir the
juices together in a tall glass.*

Rosy Pineapple Fizz

This is a reasonably mild juice which makes an
excellent sundowner.

Ingredients

An eighth of a
watermelon

Half a pineapple

Sparkling water

Crushed ice

Method

Remove the skin from the pineapple half
and chop the flesh into chunks to fit the
juicer. Cut the skin off the watermelon and
juice. Crush some ice and pour the juices
over it. Top up with sparkling water
for a long, tropical drink.

Tropical Storm

This amazingly tangy juice provides instant energy.

Ingredients

Half a pineapple

1 lime

1 grapefruit

Crushed ice

Sparkling water

Method

Remove the skin from the pineapple half and chop into chunks to fit the juicer. Peel the lime and the grapefruit. Juice the pineapple, grapefruit, and lime and pour the juices into a tall glass over the ice. Top up with sparkling water.

Mango Wine

The mango and melon combine to produce a mellow juice designed to relax even the tetchiest individual.

Ingredients

Half a Galia melon

5 oz (125 g) white grapes

Half a mango

Method

Remove the skin from the melon and scoop out the pits. Cut the mango in half and remove the skin and the stone. Juice the grapes (reserve a couple for decoration), followed by the mango and the melon. Mix the juice together and decorate the glass with a couple of grapes.

Orange Hedgerow

A tangy version of the traditional blackberry and apple concoction.

Ingredients

5 oz (125 g) blackberries

1 orange

1 apple

Method

Rinse the blackberries and juice. Peel the orange and juice it, followed by the roughly chopped apple. Stir the juices together in a glass.

Appendix: A Healthy Diet

The value of any diet depends upon a good balance of all the essential nutrients. A well-balanced diet should include the following, although specific requirements vary from person to person: vitamins A, B group, C, D, E, iron, calcium, phosphorus, magnesium, sodium, potassium, zinc, and trace elements copper, iodine, fluorine, selenium , and chromium.

Vitamins: With the exception of niacin and vitamin D, the body cannot manufacture or synthesize vitamins. They must be obtained in the diet or from supplements. Vitamins are essential to the normal functioning of our bodies and are necessary for our growth, vitality, and general well-being. Vitamins cannot replace food. In fact, they cannot be assimilated without ingesting food, which is why we suggest taking them with a meal. Vitamins help regulate metabolism, convert fat and carbohydrates into energy, and assist in forming bones and tissues. A varied diet should supply all vitamin needs. For vegans intake of vitamins B12 and D may be inadequate. These can be obtained from supplements and, in the case of vitamin D, adequate exposure to sunlight. It is difficult to overdose on vitamins, as excess will be excreted by the body.

Minerals: Again, most people obtain adequate minerals from their diet: additional amounts are not beneficial. Taken in excess some mineral supplements may be harmful. Important as vitamins are, they cannot be assimilated without the aid of minerals. Although the body can manufacture a few vitamins, it cannot manufacture a single mineral. The body's tissues and internal fluids contain varying quantities of minerals. Minerals are constituents of the bones, teeth, soft tissue, muscle, blood, and nerve cells. They are vital to overall mental and physical well-being. Minerals act as catalysts for many biological reactions within the body, including muscle response, the transmission of messages through the nervous system, the production of hormones, digestion, and the utilization of nutrients in foods. Mineral supplements are sometimes required by people who have digestive disorders that impair the absorption of certain minerals from the diet. The most commonly used supplement is iron which is used to treat iron-deficient anaemia, and is sometimes required by women who are pregnant or breastfeeding. Iron can be obtained from green leafy vegetables. Iodine is essential for the formation of thyroid hormones which control the rate of the metabolism. The level of iodine in food is reliant on the amount present in animal feed and the soil. Iodine is added to bread and salt in places where there is a risk of deficiency (this is not a common ailment). Iodine can be found in some green leafy vegetables. Calcium supplements are used during pregnancy and for young children. Calcium is essential for healthy bones and teeth. It is the most abundant mineral in the body and can be obtained from green leafy vegetables.

Trace elements: Trace elements (such as copper, iodine, fluorine, selenium, and chromium) are only required in tiny amounts and most play an essential part in the activities of several enzymes. In excess they are extremely toxic.

Fiber: In addition to the essential vitamins and minerals, a healthy diet should also include dietary fiber, which plays an role in aiding normal bowel function. Fiber can be obtained through eating unrefined carbohydrates such as cereals, root vegetables, and fruits.

Amino acids: Finally, the milk and meat groups of food also provide amino acids to our diets. Amino acids are the 'building blocks' of the body, being the constituent parts of all proteins. They have various functions: in addition to building cells and repairing tissue, they form antibodies to combat invading bacteria and viruses. They are part of the enzyme and hormonal system and are essential for the structure of nucleoproteins (RNA and DNA). When protein is broken down by digestion the result is twenty-two known amino acids. Eight are essential (cannot be manufactured by the body): tryptophan, lysine, methinine, phenylalanine, threonine, valine, luecine, and isoleucine. The rest are non-essential and can be manufactured by the body with proper nutrition.

Bibliography

Blake, Susannah, *Smoothies*, Anness Publishing, 2001

Holford, Patrick, *The Optimum Nutrition Bible*, Piatkus 1997

Holford, Patrick and Ridgway, Judy, *The Optimum Nutrition Cookbook*, Piatkus 1999

Kenton, Leslie, *The Raw Energy Bible*, Vermillion, 1996

Kenton, Leslie with Russell Cronin, *Juice High Vermillion*, 1996

Straten, Michael van, *Superjuice*, Mitchell Beazley, 1999

Straten, Michael van and Griggs, Barbara, *Superfoods*, Dorling Kindersley 1990

Wheater, Caroline, *Juicing for Health*, Thorsons, 1993

Whiteman, Kate, *Illustrated Encyclopedia Fruit Identifier*, Lorenz Books 2000

Yabsley Charmaine and Cross, Amanda, *Miracle Juices*, Hamlyn, 2001

The following websites are fruitful sources of inspiration and information.

www. biosupply. com

www. evesgarden. ca

www. godsbanquet. com

www. internethealthlibrary. com

www. living-foods. com

www. omegajuicers. com/recipes. html

www. paxuk. com

www. thejuicercompany. co. uk

www. thejuiceglass. com

vegetarian. about. com

www. vitaminb17. org

Acknowledgments

Grateful thanks to Eleanor Stillwell for casting a sceptical scientist's eye over the whole manuscript and adding some crucial information; to Karen Annan and Katie Kitchen for invaluable help and advice, and to my daughter Lizzie Millidge for inventing some excellent recipes. Many thanks also to Maria Costantino, food stylist extraordinaire.

Picture credits

Pages 22 and 33 Photographs © Photodisk, Getty Images.